Contents

Test type	Quantity	Total marks	Suggested timing	Pages
Introduction				4–5
Placement Test (A/B)	1	70	45 minutes	6–9
Vocabulary Checks (A/B)	8	15/20	15 minutes	10–25
Grammar Checks (A/B)	8	15	15 minutes	26–33
Language Tests (A/B): Vocabulary, Grammar, Communication	9	30	45 minutes	34–51
Skills Tests (A/B): Listening, Communication, Reading, Writing	4	30	45 minutes	52–67
Mid-Year Test 1–4 (A/B): Vocabulary, Grammar + Listening, Communication, Reading	1	30 + 20	45 + 35 minutes	68–71
End-of-Year Test 1–8 (A/B): Vocabulary, Grammar + Listening, Communication, Reading	1	30 + 20	45 + 35 minutes	72–75
Exam Tests 1–4: Reading & Writing, Listening & Communication	1	30	45 minutes	76–79
Exam Test 5–8: Reading & Writing, Listening & Communication	1	30	45 minutes	80–83
Speaking Tasks	4	20	5–8 minutes	84–87
Writing Tasks	8	10	10 minutes	88
Audio script				89–90
Answer key				91–95

Introduction

GoGetter Tests

This booklet contains a complete tests package for *GoGetter 3*. All of the tests are in photocopiable format. Audio for the listening tasks is available for downloading from MyEnglishLab.

Assessment of learning or Assessment for learning?

GoGetter offers a variety of tests which enable the teacher to monitor students' progress both at acquiring the new language and developing language skills. Any test can be used either as an assessment of learning or an assessment for learning. Assessment of learning usually takes place after the learning has happened and provides information about what students have achieved by giving a mark or a grade. You can also use a test as an assessment for learning by providing specific feedback on students' strengths and weaknesses, and suggestions for improvement as part of the on-going learning process. A combination of both types of assessment can be a powerful tool for helping your students to learn.

It is very important to make sure students understand the tasks in every test and explain them if necessary. Also, it is very useful for students to receive constructive feedback and be advised how they can improve.

Versions of tests

Most tests have two versions: A and B. Versions A and B feature the same task types and are designed to have the same level of difficulty. However, the test items in each version are usually different or the sequence in which they occur differs. In the listening tasks, the test items are different, but the audio is the same for both A and B versions, which makes it easy to administer a test.

You can use the tests that have two versions in two ways:

- give half the students in the class the A version and the other half the B version – this will help to deter students from cheating.
- give all students in the class the A version. You can then use the B version for students who missed the test or would like to retake it. Students who need a little more work on the unit objectives can use version B as remedial material.

Types of tests

Placement Test

The *GoGetter 3* Placement Test has been designed to help you decide which level of the *GoGetter* series, level 2, level 3 or level 4, is best suited to your students. If students score:

- 0–14 points (0–20%), we suggest they start at level 2.
- 15–28 points (21–40%), you might consider an additional oral interview to decide whether level 2 or level 3 (the latter with some remedial work) would be more appropriate.
- 29–42 points (41–60%), we suggest they start at level 3.
- 43–52 points (61–75%), you might consider an additional oral interview to decide whether level 3 or level 4 (the latter with some remedial work) would be more appropriate.
- 53–70 points (76+%), we suggest they start at level 4.

Vocabulary Checks

There are eight Vocabulary Checks. They test the key vocabulary sets taught in units 1–8 of the Students' Book. Each Vocabulary Check comprises two or three exercises. A Vocabulary Check can be administered upon completing all lessons with vocabulary input in a unit. Alternatively, it can be cut up into mini-tests and administered after completing work on the relevant vocabulary set.

Grammar Checks

There are eight Grammar Checks. They test the grammar taught in lessons 2 and 3 of units 1–8 of the Students' Book. Each Grammar Check comprises two or three exercises. A Grammar Check can be administered upon completing lesson 3 of a unit. Alternatively, it can be cut up into two mini-tests and administered after completing work on the relevant grammar point.

Language Tests

There are nine Language Tests. They test the vocabulary, grammar and language for communication taught in the *Get started!* unit and units 1–8 of the Students' Book. The tests can be administered upon completing each unit.

Skills Tests

There are four Skills Tests. Each exploits the language taught in two successive units of the Students' Book. The Skills Tests check students' progress using the following skills-based tasks: Listening, Communication, Reading and Writing. In each test one of the listening tasks and the communication task mirror the exam-style tasks used in the relevant Skills Revision section in the Students' Book. The tests can be administered upon completing units 2, 4, 6 and 8.

Mid-Year Test and End-of-Year Test

The Mid-Year Test and the End-of-Year Test have the same structure and consist of two parts. The first part, Exercises 1–6, tests the vocabulary and grammar taught in the relevant units of the Students' Book. The second part, Exercises 7–9, is skills-based and comprises Listening, Communication and Reading. The Mid-Year Test should be administered after completing the first four units of the Students' Book, and the End-of-Year Test – after all units have been completed.

Exam Tests

There are two Exam Tests. Exam Test 1–4 should be used after completing the first four units of the Students' Book including *Skills Revision*. Exam Test 5–8 should be administered after units 5–8 have been completed. The two tests mirror the Exam Practice section of the *GoGetter 3 Workbook* and comprise two sections: Reading & Writing and Listening & Communication. These tests provide the opportunity to check students' progress and proficiency through typical exam tasks similar to those in *Pearson Test of English for Young Learners* and *Cambridge English: Young Learners of English Tests* (adapted to suit this level and age group).

Speaking Tasks

There are four sets of Speaking Tasks, each enabling you to test the material from two successive units. Each set has visual material for the student and notes for the teacher at the bottom of the page, which should be cut off along the dotted line. There are two tasks in the notes for the teacher:

- Task 1: elicitation of the vocabulary illustrated,
- Task 2: asking and answering personalised questions related to both the picture and the student's experience.

The student should respond using structures and vocabulary from the relevant units.

The Speaking Tasks can complement the respective Skills Tests, Mid-Year Test and End-of-Year Test or be administered separately. The following marking criteria and evaluation scales will help you mark consistently and give students meaningful feedback.

Marking criteria

- 0–5 points for the range of language used (structures and vocabulary). See the list of target structures and vocabulary for each Speaking Task in the notes for the teacher.
- 0–5 points for accuracy of expression
- 0–5 points for fluency
- 0–5 points for pronunciation

Evaluation scales	Language range	Accuracy	Fluency	Pronunciation
Excellent 18–20 points	The student commands a full range of the vocabulary and grammar taught and uses it appropriately.	The student makes no or very few mistakes.	The student speaks fluently, with no hesitation. He/She can use full sentences. Students should not be penalised for using single words or phrases where appropriate.	The student's pronunciation is clear and accurate.
Good 15–17 points	The student commands a good range of the vocabulary and grammar taught.	The student makes mistakes occasionally.	The student speaks fluently, with little hesitation. He/She can use full sentences. Students should not be penalised for using single words or phrases where appropriate.	The student's pronunciation is clear and accurate most of the time.
Satisfactory 10–14 points	The student can use some of the basic vocabulary and grammar taught.	The student makes mistakes but these do not prevent communication.	The student speaks with some hesitation because he/she is trying to think of the right words. He/She answers using full sentences some of the time but clearly prefers using phrases.	The student's pronunciation is clear on the whole; occasional poor pronunciation does not prevent communication.
Unsatisfactory 6–9 points	The student can use very little vocabulary and grammar.	The student makes a lot of mistakes which hinder good communication. He/She is able to communicate successfully at least once.	The student hesitates frequently because he/she cannot think of the right words. He/She answers using mainly phrases or single words.	The student's pronunciation is poor and makes communication difficult.
Very poor 0–5 points	The student gives no answer or knows only a few basic words.	The student is unable to communicate or gives inaccurate answers that prevent communication.	The student cannot think of the right words and says very little.	The student gives no answer or can pronounce fairly correctly only a few words.

Writing Tasks

There are eight Writing Tasks corresponding to Units 1–8 in the Students' Book. You can use the tasks as in-class writing tests or assign them as homework.

Each writing task contains a topic, several questions that students are asked to refer to or prompts they are asked to use in their works and a word limit. The tasks for all units have a 70–80-word limit.

The following marking criteria and evaluation scales are provided to help you mark consistently and to give students meaningful feedback.

Marking criteria

- 0–5 points for content. Award 5 marks if the student refers to all the questions connected with the topic.
- 1 point for not going under or over the word limit
- 2 points for accuracy of expression
- 2 points for the range of language used. See the Marking check lists and model texts for each writing task on page 95 of this booklet.

Evaluation scales

Excellent:	9–10 points
Good:	7–8 points
Satisfactory:	5–6 points
Unsatisfactory:	3–4 points
Very poor:	0–2 points

Tests on MyEnglishLab

Visit www.MyEnglishLab.com to access the following:

- online versions of Skills Tests, Mid-Year Test and End-of-Year Test, which can be assigned to your students and automatically checked,
- *GoGetter Tests* in PDF and editable format, and audio for tests,
- PDF versions of *GoGetter Tests* adjusted to the needs of dyslectic students.

Use the Teacher Access Code to unlock the teacher content on MyEnglishLab. You will find the code and registration details in *GoGetter* Teacher's Book.

Placement Test A

name _____ class _____

Vocabulary

1 Circle the odd one out.

0 calculator	(library)	ruler	dictionary
1 canteen	rubber	gym	playground
2 cereal	cheese	jar	fruit
3 meat	printer	screen	keyboard
4 builder	nurse	vet	tablet
5 tram	island	train	underground
6 forest	hospital	theatre	stadium

☐ / ⑥

2 Complete the sentences with the verbs in the box.

chat do get look make ~~take~~ visit

0 *Take* a photo of your family.
1 They _____ online with their friends every day.
2 Jim and I _____ our beds in the morning.
3 We _____ ballet on Monday and Thursday.
4 _____ off the bus at the next bus stop.
5 Let's _____ this museum.
6 I sometimes _____ after my little sister.

☐ / ⑥

3 Circle the correct answer.

0 Please don't forget to ____ the dog.
  a go   (b) feed   c water
1 I always ____ the table after we have dinner.
  a clear   b load   c set
2 Please come home before it gets ____.
  a lost   b dark   c bored
3 They wake ____ very early in the morning.
  a out   b on   c up
4 I always give Granny ____ when I see her.
  a a hug   b a call   c hands
5 I'd like to live ____ when I'm older.
  a a family   b my own business
  c abroad
6 I love the sea. I want to go ____ tomorrow.
  a snorkelling   b camping   c hiking

☐ / ⑥

4 Circle the correct word.

0 Let's go shopping, but let's make a shopping (list) / basket first.
1 'I haven't got any money.' 'That's OK. I can pay by cash / card.'
2 Let's buy some vegetables at the greengrocer's / newsagent's.
3 Peel / Beat the apples and slice them.
4 Put some yoghurt and fruit in the console / blender to make a smoothie.
5 I was frying potatoes when I got this cut / burn.
6 It's a nice day. Let's eat lunch outside on the attic / balcony.
7 Please, put the dirty plates in the sink / cupboard.

☐ / ⑦

Grammar

5 Complete the sentences with the Present Simple or the Present Continuous form of the verbs.

0 The students *do* (do) their homework every day.
1 He _____ (watch) TV at the moment.
2 Hannah usually _____ (study) in her bedroom.
3 I _____ (know) the answers to all the questions.
4 We _____ (not visit) Grandma on Sundays.
5 What _____ (they / make) for lunch today?
6 _____ (Amy / play) the piano every day?
7 I _____ (not work) in the garden at the moment.

☐ / ⑦

6 Circle the correct answer.

0 Your idea is good / (better) than Julia's.
1 Please speak quiet / quietly in the library.
2 How much / many sugar is there in the packet?
3 I haven't got some / any interesting books to read.
4 I can't eat the food. It's enough / too hot.
5 The Nile is longest / the longest river in the world.
6 Adam isn't as organised / more organised as Betty.
7 'Who / Whose backpack is that?' 'It's Anna's backpack.'

☐ / ⑦

© Pearson Education Limited 2019 | PHOTOCOPIABLE

Placement Test A

name ______________________ class ________

7 Complete the sentences with the Past Simple form of the verbs.

0 I *finished* (finish) my homework an hour ago.
1 The weather ____________ (not be) good yesterday.
2 We ____________ (not study) French last year.
3 He ____________ (go) to Spain two years ago.
4 There ____________ (be) a lot of people at the party.
5 ____________ (you / make) this cake? It's delicious!
6 She ____________ (meet) her friends yesterday.
7 ____________ (you / be) tired after your walk?

☐ / [7]

8 Circle the correct answer.

0 I *waited* / (*was waiting*) for a bus when I saw the accident.
1 What *were you* / *you were* doing yesterday at four o'clock?
2 Have you ever *stay* / *stayed* in a hotel?
3 Mum *have* / *has* made a cake for me.
4 I have *ever* / *never* tried Mexican food.
5 You *should* / *shouldn't* leave your rubbish on the beach.
6 We *can* / *must* be quiet when the baby is sleeping.
7 You *must* / *mustn't* play football in the street. It's dangerous!

☐ / [7]

9 Complete the sentences with the words in the box.

are doesn't to going ~~having~~ has will won't

0 We are *having* a party this evening.
1 When ________ you going to visit us?
2 I hope I ________ pass my exams.
3 Why do you have ________ go so soon?
4 It's a holiday. Dad ________ have to work today.
5 I think children ________ go to school in the future. They'll learn at home.
6 Mum is ________ to make a delicious salad for dinner.
7 Janet ________ to get up very early on Mondays.

☐ / [7]

Communication

10 Complete the dialogues with the words and phrases in the box.

a moment can I borrow here you are in my opinion ~~where~~ would you like

0 A: *Where* do you live?
B: In London.
1 A: What ____________?
B: Can I have a pizza, please?
2 A: Hello, it's Lily here. Can I speak to Mike, please?
B: Just ____________.
3 A: What do you think of these comic books?
B: ____________ they're fantastic!
4 A: ____________ your phone, please?
B: Sure. No problem.
5 A: I'd like a ticket to Birmingham, please.
B: ____________. That's £12.30.

☐ / [5]

11 Match 1–5 with replies a–f. There is one extra reply.

0 Would you like to go to the cinema with me? [g]
1 Can you help me with my homework, please? ☐
2 You look upset. What happened? ☐
3 I've got a headache. ☐
4 Would you like to watch a DVD or play a game? ☐
5 Do you have these trousers in blue? ☐

a I don't mind. You choose.
b I lost my keys this morning.
c I'm sorry, I can't. I'm busy right now.
d I don't agree with you.
e Sorry, we don't.
f Why don't you lie down?
g That sounds fun. Thank you.

☐ / [5]

Vocabulary	☐ / [25]	Communication	☐ / [10]
Grammar	☐ / [35]	**Your total score**	☐ / [70]

© Pearson Education Limited 2019 PHOTOCOPIABLE

Placement Test B

© Pearson Education Limited 2019 PHOTOCOPIABLE

name _____   class _____

Vocabulary

1 Circle the odd one out.

0	calculator	(library)	ruler	dictionary
1	hospital	train	tram	underground
2	cheese	meat	carton	yoghurt
3	farmer	pilot	nurse	keyboard
4	cereal	printer	screen	mouse
5	gym	laptop	canteen	playground
6	beach	forest	bank	volcano

☐ / ⑥

2 Complete the sentences with the verbs in the box.

do get stay ~~take~~ text tidy walk

0 *Take* a photo of your family.

1 We _____ karate on Tuesday and Friday.

2 Let's _____ in this hotel.

3 I _____ my dog every morning.

4 _____ on the train and sit down.

5 They _____ their friends all the time.

6 Tim and I _____ our bedroom every weekend.

☐ / ⑥

3 Circle the correct answer.

0 Please don't forget to ____ the dog.
   a go   **(b)**feed   **c** water

1 I always ____ the table for breakfast.
   a make   **b** load   **c** set

2 I must look ____ my keys. I can't find them.
   a out   **b** for   **c** on

3 Be polite and ____ hands when you meet people.
   a ask   **b** shake   **c** give

4 Don't get ____. Take a map with you.
   a lost   **b** dark   **c** bored

5 I love sleeping in a tent. I want to go ____.
   a cycling   **b** snorkelling   **c** camping

6 I'd like to have ____ one day.
   a abroad   **b** my own business   **c** famous

☐ / ⑥

4 Circle the correct word.

0 Let's go shopping, but let's make a shopping (list)/ basket first.

1 Buy some oranges at the *newsagent's / greengrocer's*.

2 Put the clean plates in the *cupboard / sink*.

3 It's a nice day. Let's eat lunch outside on the *balcony / basement*.

4 *Beat / Peel* the carrots and chop them.

5 I was slicing bread, when I got this *cut / bite*.

6 'I haven't got any money.' 'That's OK. I can pay by *card / cash*.'

7 Let's put some yoghurt and fruit in the *blender / player* and make a smoothie.

☐ / ⑦

Grammar

5 Complete the sentences with the Present Simple or the Present Continuous form of the verbs.

0 The students *do* (do) their homework every day.

1 They _____ (not get) up early on Sundays.

2 She _____ (have) a shower at the moment.

3 I _____ (want) to play a computer game now.

4 _____ (Max / play) football every weekend?

5 What _____ (you / watch) on TV right now?

6 I _____ (not help) Mum in the garden at the moment.

7 Brian usually _____ (study) in the living room.

☐ / ⑦

6 Circle the correct answer.

0 Your idea is *good /*(*better*)than Julia's.

1 '*Whose / Who* pencil case is that?' 'It's Alan's pencil case.'

2 I haven't got *any / some* interesting films to watch.

3 How *much / many* milk is there in the fridge?

4 Mia isn't *as patient / more patient* as Peter.

5 Please speak *quiet / quietly* in the library.

6 I can't wear this coat. It's *too / enough* small.

7 August is *hottest / the hottest* month in my country.

☐ / ⑦

Placement Test B

name ______________________ class ________

7 Complete the sentences with the Past Simple form of the verbs.

0 I *finished* (finish) my homework an hour ago.
1 She ____________ (go) to Italy two years ago.
2 ________________ (you / eat) all the cakes?
3 The weather ____________ (not be) nice last week.
4 There ____________ (be) a lot of people on the beach.
5 He ____________ (make) a delicious cake yesterday.
6 ____________ (you / be) late for school this morning?
7 We ____________________ (not study) Maths yesterday.

[ ] / [7]

8 Circle the correct answer.

0 I *waited* / *was waiting* for a bus when I saw the accident.
1 What *you were* / *were you* doing yesterday at five o'clock?
2 Have you ever *try* / *tried* Chinese food?
3 I have *never* / *ever* stayed in a hotel.
4 Dad *have* / *has* made pancakes for dinner.
5 You *must* / *mustn't* make a noise. The baby is sleeping.
6 You *can* / *must* be careful when you cross the street.
7 You *should* / *shouldn't* leave your rubbish in the forest.

[ ] / [7]

9 Complete the sentences with the words in the box.

are doesn't to going ~~having~~ has will won't

0 We are *having* a party this evening.
1 Dad ________ to get up early on weekdays.
2 When ________ you going to see the dentist?
3 I think children ________ go to school in the future. They'll learn at home.
4 It's Sunday. Mum ________ have to work today.
5 What time do you have ________ leave?
6 I hope I ________ be happy in the future.
7 Alan is ________ to study French next year.

[ ] / [7]

Communication

10 Complete the dialogues with the words and phrases in the box.

here you are I'm afraid in my opinion is it OK ~~where~~ would you like

0 A: *Where* do you live?
B: In London.
1 A: ________________ the film isn't very good.
B: You're right. It's silly.
2 A: We'd like two tickets to Edinburgh, please.
B: ________________. That's £46.50.
3 A: ________________ anything to drink?
B: No, thank you.
4 A: ________________ if I use your phone?
B: Yes, that's fine.
5 A: Hello, it's Mark here. Can I speak to Fiona, please?
B: ________________ she's out.

[ ] / [5]

11 Match 1–5 with replies a–f. There is one extra reply.

0 Would you like to go to the cinema with me? [g]
1 Do you have this hoodie in red? [ ]
2 You look worried. What happened? [ ]
3 Would you like to listen to music or watch a DVD? [ ]
4 Can you help me with the cooking, please? [ ]
5 I've got a stomachache. [ ]

a Why don't you drink some mint tea?
b I dropped my phone and it stopped working.
c I don't mind. You choose.
d Sorry, we don't.
e I disagree with you.
f I'm sorry, I can't. I'm busy right now.
g That sounds great. Thank you.

[ ] / [5]

Vocabulary	[ ] / [25]	Communication	[ ] / [10]
Grammar	[ ] / [35]	**Your total score**	[ ] / [70]

© Pearson Education Limited 2019 PHOTOCOPIABLE

1 Vocabulary Check A

name ______________________ class ______

1.1 Household chores

A

1 Look at the pictures and write the verbs.

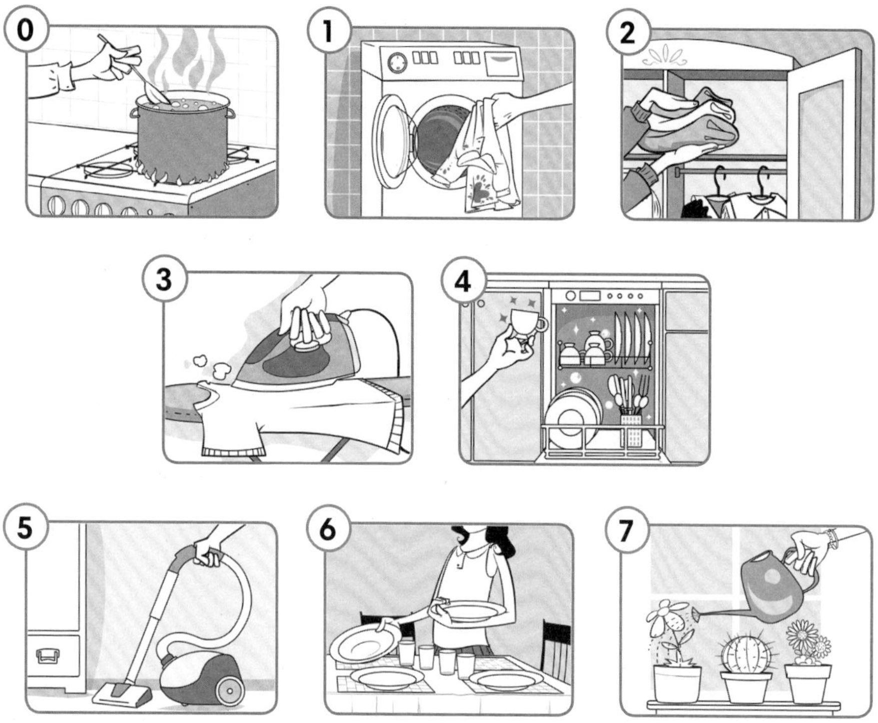

0 cook dinner
1 __________ the washing machine
2 __________ away your clothes
3 __________ your T-shirt
4 __________ the dishwasher
5 __________ your room
6 __________ the table
7 __________ the plants

[ ] / 7

2 Match 1–5 to a–e.

Everyone in Mike's family does chores.

0 He takes out [f]
1 He makes [ ]
2 He feeds [ ]
3 He clears [ ]
4 He loads [ ]
5 He hangs out [ ]

a the table after dinner.
b the washing.
c his bed every morning.
d the dishwasher.
e his dog.
f the rubbish.

[ ] / 5

© Pearson Education Limited 2019 PHOTOCOPIABLE

name ______________________ class ______

1.5 Personality adjectives

A

3 Complete the sentences with personality adjectives.

0 Sue likes helping other people. She's h e l p f u l.
1 Beth shouts a lot! She's l _ _ d.
2 Jane doesn't talk a lot. She's q _ _ _ t.
3 Amy doesn't often worry or get angry. She's e _ _ _ - _ _ _ _ g.
4 Rose likes telling other people what to do. She's b _ _ _ y.
5 Olivia never tidies her room. She's m _ _ _ y.
6 Carol makes plans and can always find things. She's o _ _ _ _ _ _ _ _ d.
7 Martha always puts things in the right place and her room is clean. She's t _ _ y.
8 Jack is a good teacher. He explains things again and again. He's p _ _ _ _ _ t.

[ ] / 8

Your total score [ ] / 20

1 Vocabulary Check B

name ______________________ class ______

1.1 Household chores

B

1 Look at the pictures and write the verbs.

0 *cook* dinner
1 __________ your room
2 __________ your T-shirt
3 __________ the washing machine
4 __________ the table
5 __________ away your clothes
6 __________ the plants
7 __________ the dishwasher

☐ / 7

2 Match 1–5 to a–f.

Everyone in Jenny's family does chores.

0 She takes out [*f*]
1 She clears [ ]
2 She loads [ ]
3 She makes [ ]
4 She hangs out [ ]
5 She feeds [ ]

a her dog.
b the dishwasher.
c her bed every morning.
d the washing.
e the table after breakfast.
f the rubbish.

☐ / 5

name ______________________ class ______

1.5 Personality adjectives

B

3 Complete the sentences with personality adjectives.

0 Tim likes helping other people. He's **h***e l p f u***l**.
1 Mike likes telling other people what to do. He's **b** _ _ _ **y**.
2 Luis makes plans and he can always find things. He's **o** _ _ _ _ _ _ _ **d**.
3 Sue is a good teacher. She explains things again and again. She's **p** _ _ _ _ _ **t**.
4 Mark doesn't talk a lot. He's **q** _ _ _ **t**.
5 Bill shouts a lot! He's **l** _ _ **d**.
6 Jim always puts things in the right place and he has a clean room. He's **t** _ _ **y**.
7 Thomas never tidies his room. He's **m** _ _ _ **y**.
8 Adam doesn't often worry or get angry. He's **e** _ _ _ - _ _ _ _ _ **g**.

☐ / 8

Your total score ☐ / 20

© Pearson Education Limited 2019 PHOTOCOPIABLE

2 Vocabulary Check A

name _____   class _____

2.1 Shopping

A

1 Look at the pictures and write the words.

> cashier   shopping bag   shopping basket   shopping list   shopping trolley   special offer   ~~supermarket~~

0

supermarket

1

_____

2

_____

3

BUY 1 GET 1 FREE!

_____

4

_____

5

_____

6

_____

☐ / 6

2 Complete the text.

> At the supermarket, Mum always checks the **0**p _r i c e_ of things before she buys them. Then we stand in a queue and Mum pays for the **1**s _ _ _ _ _ _ _ . She never pays by **2**c _ _ _ . She always pays in **3**c _ _ _ . She gets her **4**c _ _ _ _ _ _ and the **5**r _ _ _ _ _ _ from the person at the check-out. Then we **6**c _ _ _ _ _ the shopping to the car and go home.

☐ / 6

- -

name _____   class _____

2.3 Shops

A

3 Where can you buy these things? Write the names of the shops.

0 clothes, chairs, toys, birthday cards	d _e p a r t m e n t_ s _t o r e_
1 tennis rackets, roller skates, footballs	s _ _ _ _ _ _ s _ _ _
2 toothpaste, vitamins	c _ _ _ _ _ _ _ _ ' _
3 shoes, boots, trainers	s _ _ _ s _ _ _ _
4 books	b _ _ _ _ _ _ _
5 bread, cakes, pies	b _ _ _ _ _ ' _
6 newspapers, magazines, sweets	n _ _ _ _ _ _ _ _ _ ' _
7 oranges, apples, potatoes, tomatoes	g _ _ _ _ _ _ _ _ _ _ ' _
8 dresses, jackets, tops, jeans	c _ _ _ _ _ _ _ s _ _ _

☐ / 8

Your total score ☐ / 20

© Pearson Education Limited 2019   PHOTOCOPIABLE

2 Vocabulary Check B

name _____   class ____

2.1 Shopping

B

1 Look at the pictures and write the words.

| cashier   shopping bag   shopping basket   shopping list   shopping trolley   special offer   ~~supermarket~~ |

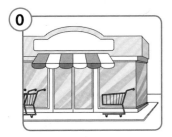   

0 supermarket

☐ / ⑥

2 Complete the text.

At the supermarket, Dad always checks the **0**p _r i c e_ of things before he buys
them. Then we **1**s _ _ _ _ in a queue with lots of other people and Dad pays for
the **2**s _ _ _ _ _ _ _ _. He never pays in **3**c _ _ _ _. He always pays by **4**c _ _ _ _.
He gets his **5**r _ _ _ _ _ _ from the person at the check-out. Then we **6**c _ _ _ _ _
the shopping to the car and go home.

☐ / ⑥

- -

name _____   class ____

2.3 Shops

B

3 Where can you buy these things? Write the names of the shops.

0 clothes, chairs, toys, birthday cards	d _e p a r t m e n t_ s _t o r e_
1 magazines, newspapers, sweets	n _ _ _ _ _ _ _ _ _ _ ' _
2 vitamins, toothpaste	c _ _ _ _ _ _ _ _ '
3 bread, pies, cakes	b _ _ _ _ _ ' _
4 dresses, jackets, tops, jeans	c _ _ _ _ _ _ _ s _ _ _ _
5 potatoes, tomatoes, apples, oranges	g _ _ _ _ _ _ _ _ _ _ _ ' _
6 footballs, tennis rackets, roller skates	s _ _ _ _ _ _ s _ _ _ _
7 books	b _ _ _ _ _ _ _ _
8 boots, trainers, shoes	s _ _ _ _ s _ _ _ _

☐ / ⑧

Your total score ☐ / ⑳

© Pearson Education Limited 2019   PHOTOCOPIABLE

3 Vocabulary Check A

name ______________________ class ______

3.1 Going on holiday **A**

1 Look at the pictures and complete the phrases.

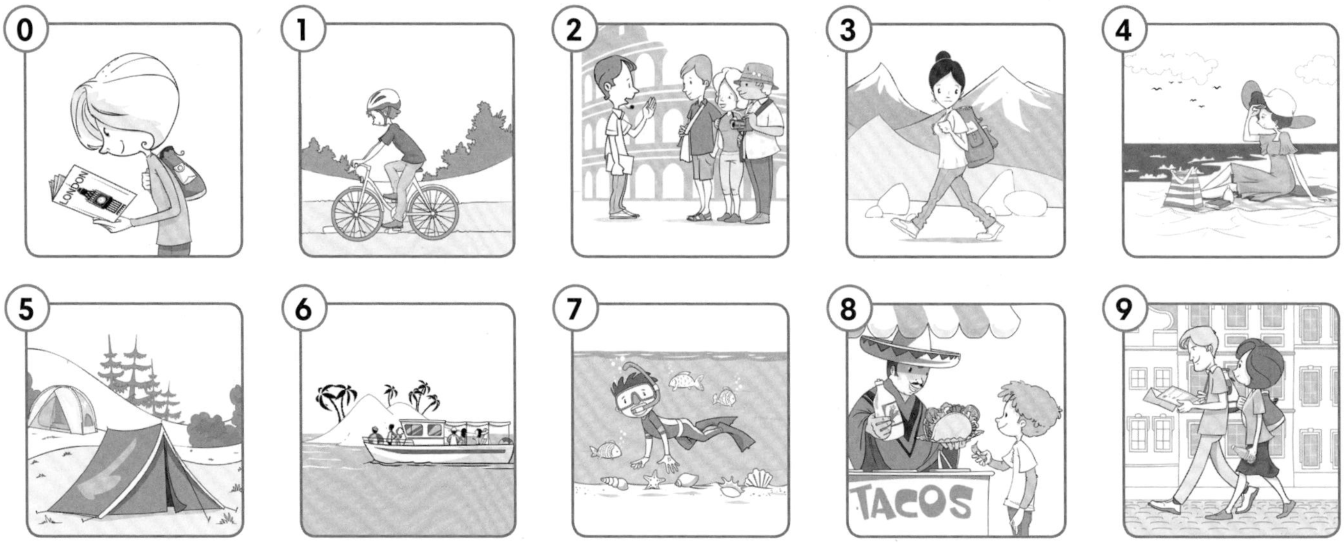

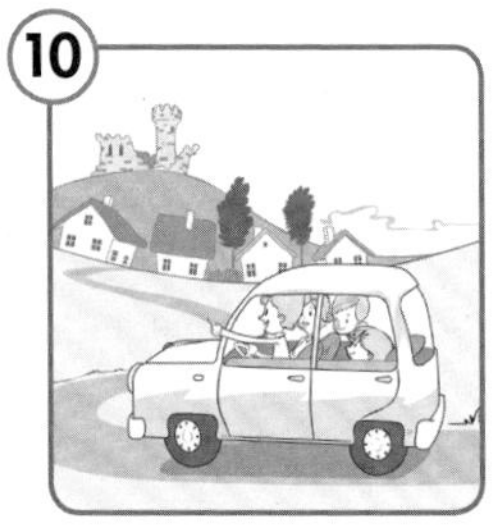

0 read a **g***uidebook*
1 go **c**_ _ _ _ _ _ _
2 go on a **g**_ _ _ _ _ _ **t**_ _ _
3 go **h**_ _ _ _ _
4 go to the **b**_ _ _ _
5 go **c**_ _ _ _ _ _ _
6 go on a **b**_ _ _ **t**_ _ _
7 go **s**_ _ _ _ _ _ _ _ _ _ _ _
8 **t**_ _ the local **f**_ _ _
9 **e**_ _ _ _ _ _ _ a city
10 go on a **d**_ _ **t**_ _ _

☐ / 10

name ______________________ class ______

3.5 Phrases with *get* **A**

2 Look at the pictures and complete the sentences with the words in the box.

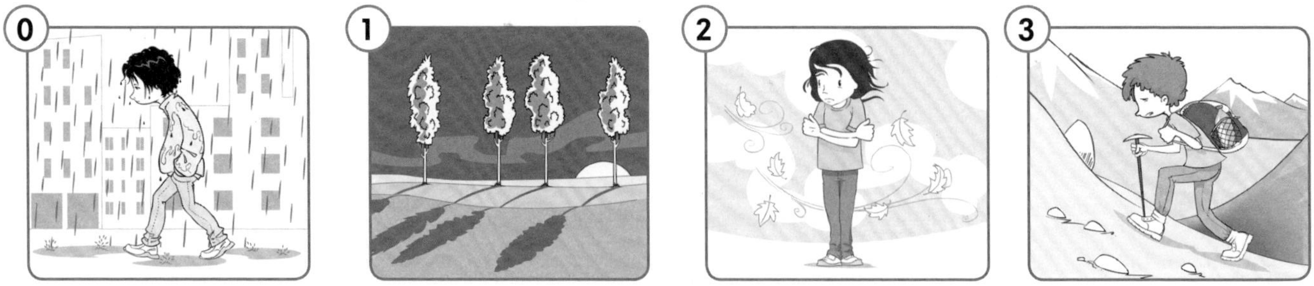

bored cold dark lost tired ~~wet~~

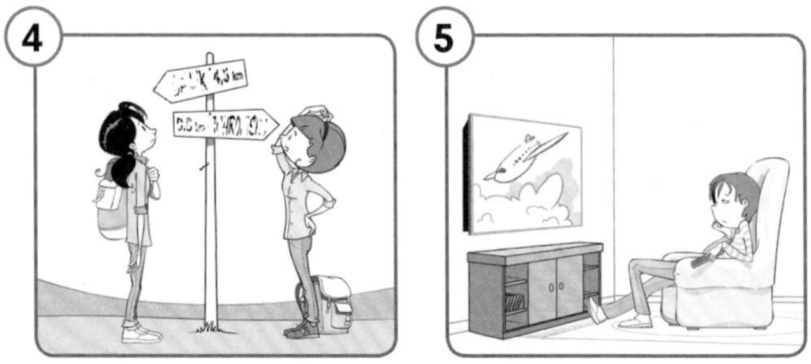

0 Tim is getting *wet* because he hasn't got an umbrella.
1 It's late and it's getting __________.
2 Lisa needs a jacket, because it's getting __________.
3 Jamie is getting __________ and he wants to rest.
4 Kate and Stella went for a walk and got __________.
5 Fred sits in front of the TV all day and he gets __________.

☐ / 5

Your total score ☐ / 15

PHOTOCOPIABLE © Pearson Education Limited 2019

3 Vocabulary Check B

name ______________________ class ____

3.1 Going on holiday

B

1 Look at the pictures and complete the phrases.

0 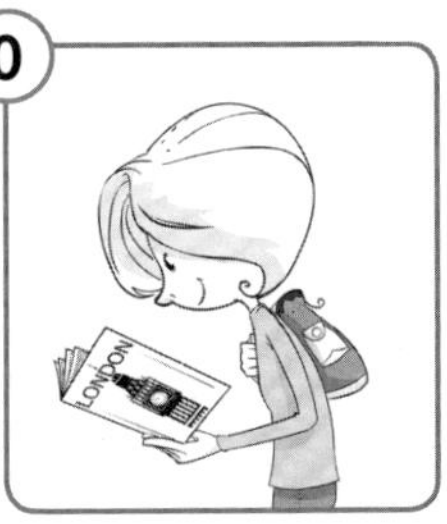
1 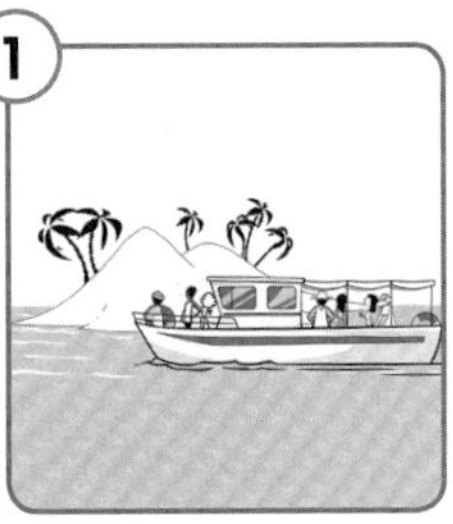
2 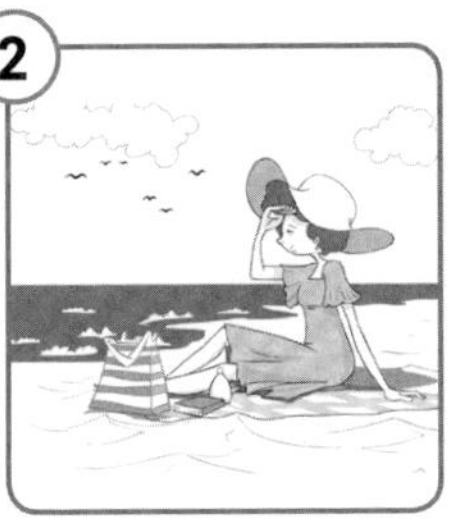
3 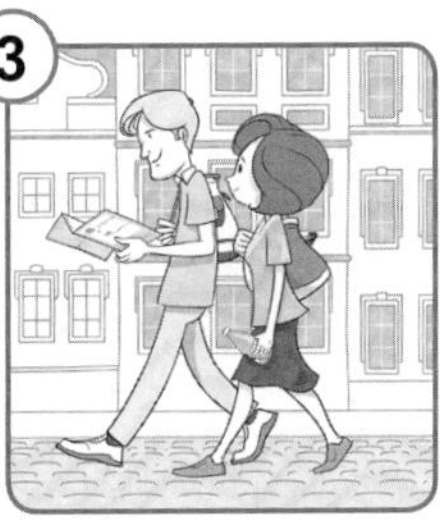
4 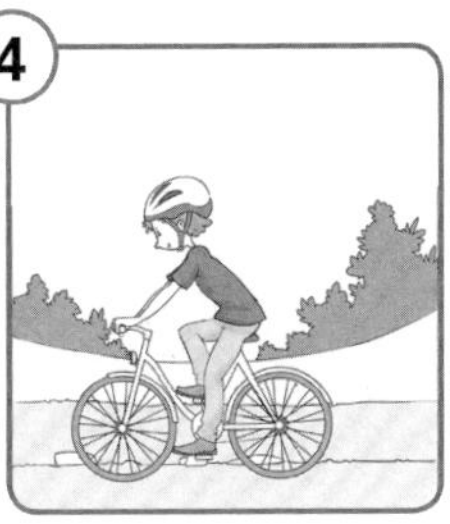
5 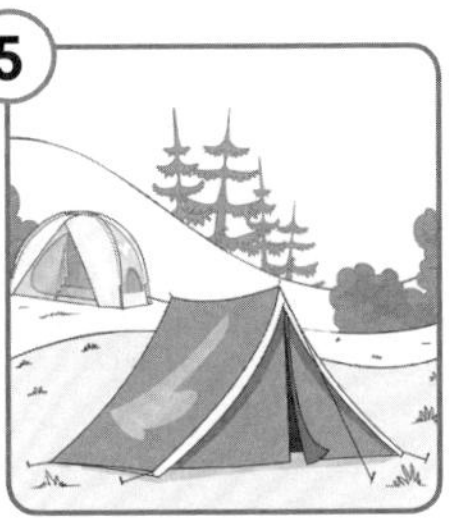
6 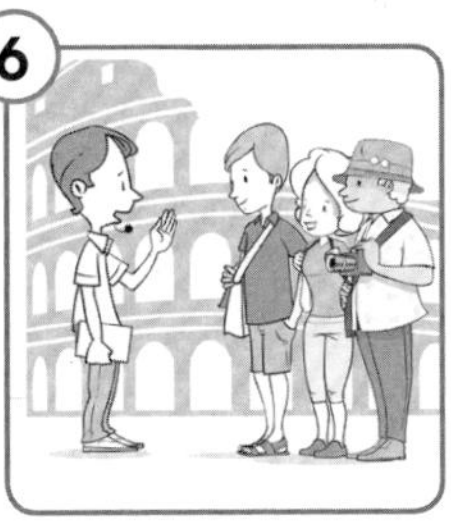
7 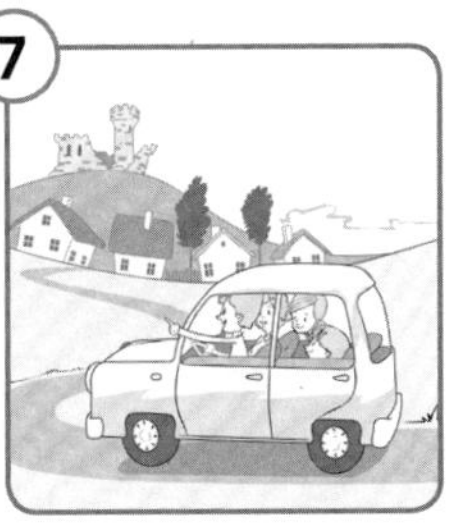
8 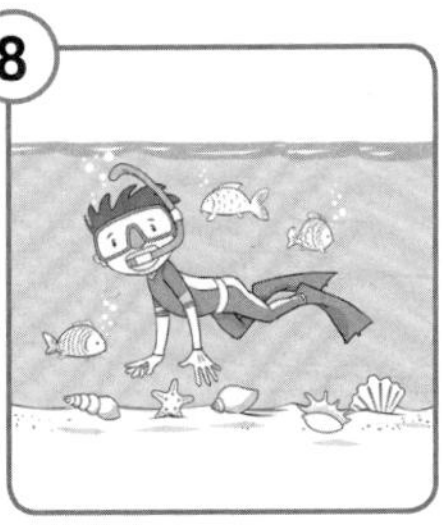
9 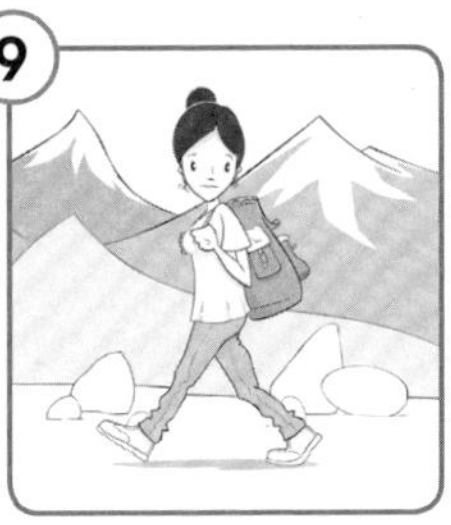
10 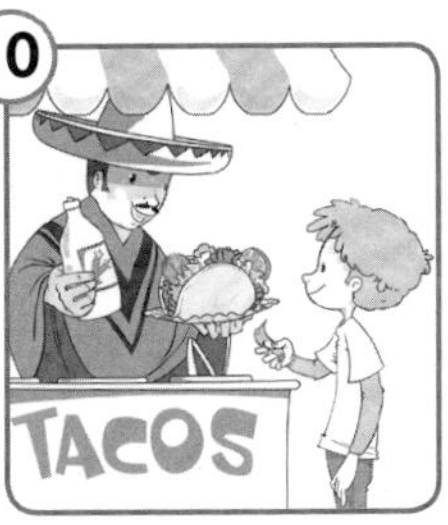

0 read a **g** *u i d e b o o k*
1 go on a **b** _ _ _ **t** _ _ _
2 go to the **b** _ _ _ _
3 **e** _ _ _ _ _ _ _ a city
4 go **c** _ _ _ _ _ _ _
5 go **c** _ _ _ _ _ _ _
6 go on a **g** _ _ _ _ _ _ **t** _ _ _
7 go on a **d** _ _ **t** _ _ _
8 go **s** _ _ _ _ _ _ _ _ _ _ _
9 go **h** _ _ _ _ _
10 **t** _ _ the local **f** _ _ _

[ ] / 10

name ______________________ class ____

3.5 Phrases with *get*

B

2 Look at the pictures and complete the sentences with the words in the box.

0 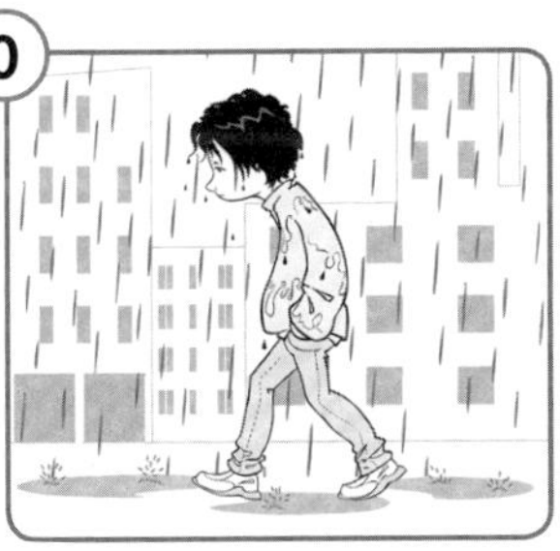
1 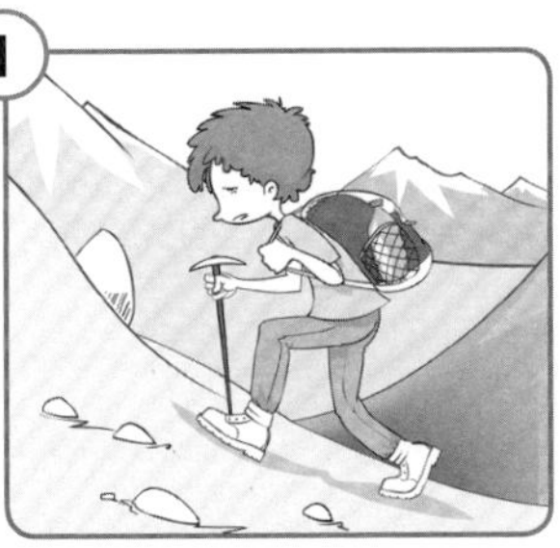
2 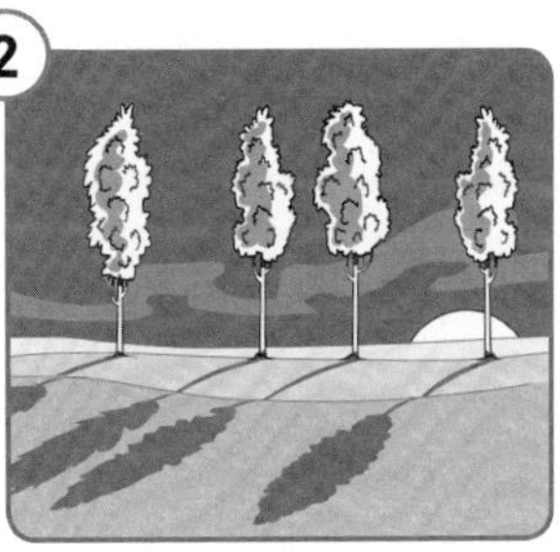
3 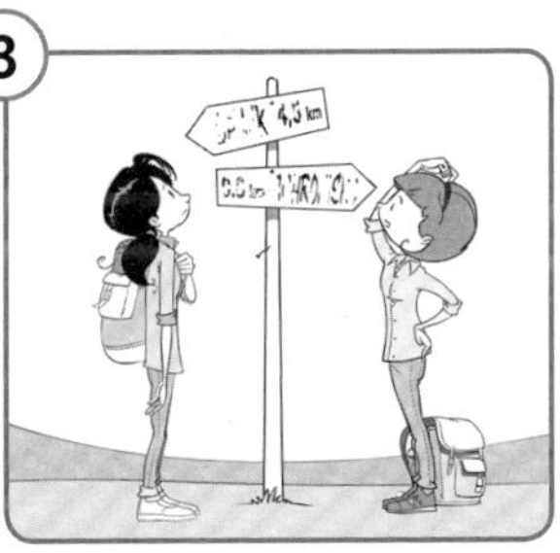

bored cold dark lost tired ~~wet~~

4 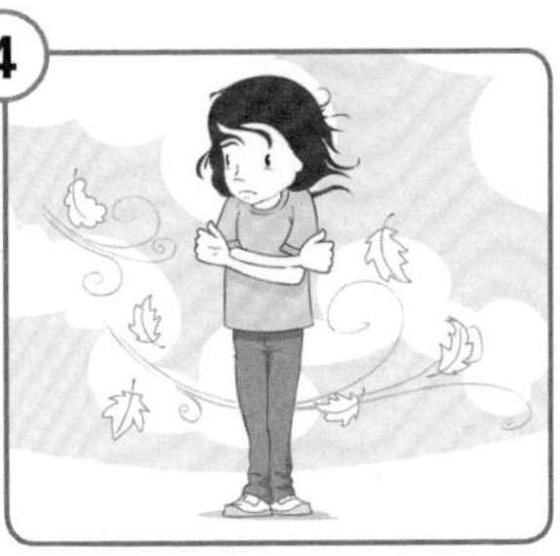
5 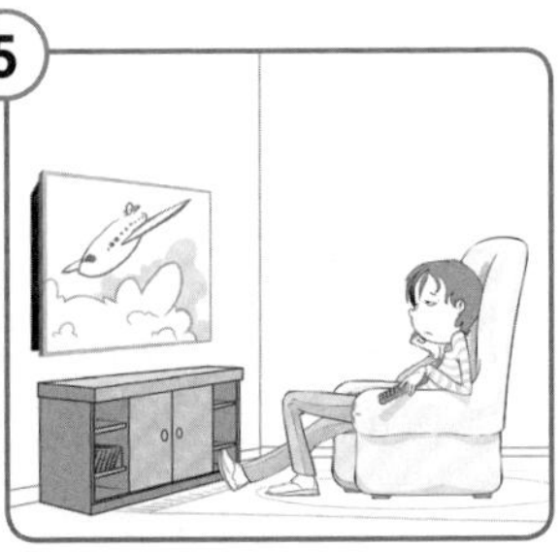

0 Tim is getting *wet* because he hasn't got an umbrella.
1 Alfie wants to rest. He is getting __________.
2 It's late and it's getting __________.
3 Jane and Lily went for a walk and got __________.
4 It's getting __________. Sarah needs a jumper.
5 Mark gets __________ because he sits in front of the TV all day.

[ ] / 5

Your total score [ ] / 15

© Pearson Education Limited 2019 PHOTOCOPIABLE

name _____ class _____

4.1 Useful things

A

1 Label the pictures.

0 p _r_ _i_ _n_ _t_ _e_ r
1 s _ _ _ t TV
2 DVD p _ _ _ _ _ r
3 USB s _ _ _ k
4 h _ _ _ _ _ _ _ _ r
5 e _ _ _ _ _ _ _ c t _ _ _ _ _ _ _ _ _ h
6 r _ _ _ _ _ e c _ _ _ _ _ _ l
7 g _ _ _ s c _ _ _ _ _ e
8 b _ _ _ _ _ _ r
9 t _ _ _ _ _ _ r
10 m _ _ _ _ _ _ _ _ _ e o _ _ n

☐ / ⑩

---

name _____ class _____

4.2 Using technology

A

2 Complete the sentences with the words in the box.

| in off on ~~press~~ unplug |

0 _Press_ this button to start the laptop.
1 Please turn _____ the lights before you go to bed.
2 _____ the fridge, please. I want to empty it and clean it.
3 Plug _____ the computer and connect to the Internet.
4 Please turn _____ the radio. I want to listen to the football results.

☐ / ④

---

name _____ class _____

4.5 Smartphones

A

3 Circle the correct answer.

0 Where are my (headphones) / ringtones? It's late but I want to listen to music.
1 Your phone isn't working because the *battery* / *app* is at 0%!
2 Is that your *portable charger* / *ringtone*? It's my favourite song!
3 You can download this useful *Wi-Fi* / *app* to your phone or computer.
4 Is there *Wi-Fi* / *battery* here? I want to connect to the Internet.
5 Wash your hands before you put your fingers on the *app* / *touch screen*.
6 Take a *portable charger* / *mouse* with you so you can use your laptop for more hours.

☐ / ⑥

© Pearson Education Limited 2019 | PHOTOCOPIABLE

Your total score ☐ / ⑳

4 Vocabulary Check B

name _____   class _____

4.1 Useful things

B

1 Label the pictures.

0 p _r_ _i_ _n_ _t_ _e_ r
1 USB s _ _ _ _ k
2 DVD p _ _ _ _ _ r
3 t _ _ _ _ _ _ r
4 g _ _ _ s c _ _ _ _ _ _ e
5 s _ _ _ t TV
6 e _ _ _ _ _ _ _ c t _ _ _ _ _ _ _ _ _ h
7 h _ _ _ _ _ _ _ _ r
8 m _ _ _ _ _ _ _ _ _ e o _ _ n
9 b _ _ _ _ _ _ r
10 r _ _ _ _ _ e c _ _ _ _ _ _ l

☐ / ⑩

© Pearson Education Limited 2019   PHOTOCOPIABLE

---

name _____   class _____

4.2 Using technology

B

2 Complete the sentences with the words in the box.

> in off on ~~press~~ unplug

0 _Press_ this button to start the laptop.
1 _____ the fridge, please. I want to empty it and clean it.
2 Please turn _____ the radio. I want to listen to the football results.
3 Please turn _____ the lights before you go to bed.
4 Plug _____ the computer and connect to the Internet

☐ / ④

---

name _____   class _____

4.5 Smartphones

B

3 Circle the correct answer.

0 Where are my (headphones) / ringtones? It's late but I want to listen to music.
1 Is there _battery / Wi-Fi_ here? I want to connect to the Internet.
2 I always take a _touch screen / portable charger_ with me so I can use my tablet for more hours.
3 His _ringtone / battery_ is his favourite song.
4 Don't put your dirty fingers on your _app / touch screen_. Wash your hands first.
5 My phone isn't working because the _mouse / battery_ is at 0%!
6 This is a useful _app / Wi-Fi_ and you can download it to your phone or computer.

☐ / ⑥

Your total score ☐ / ⑳

17

5 Vocabulary Check A

name ______________________ class ____

5.1 Health problems

A

1 Look at the pictures and complete the sentences.

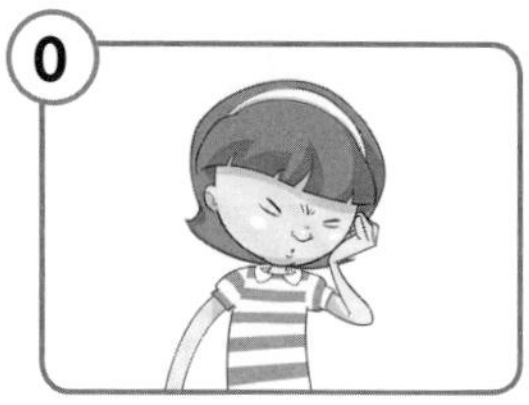

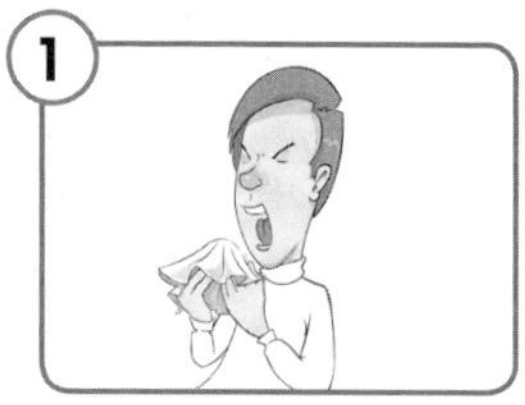

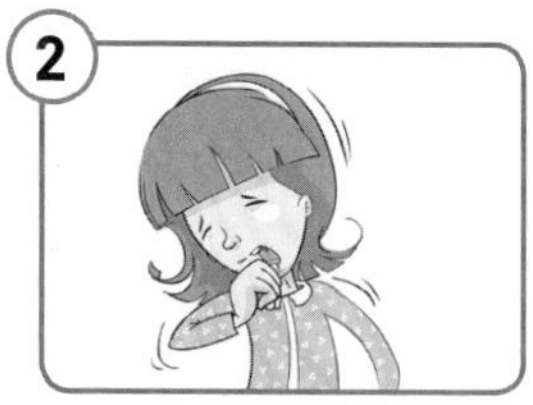

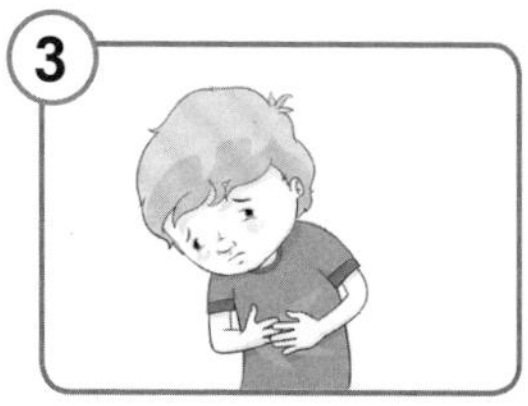

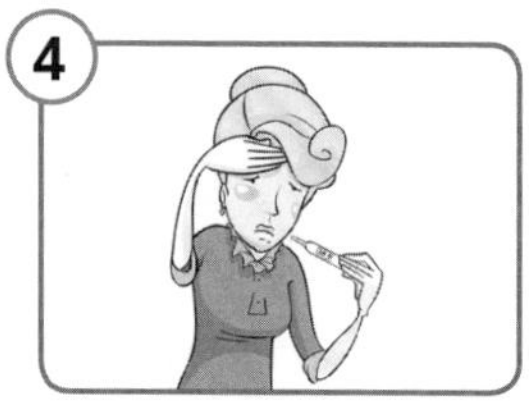

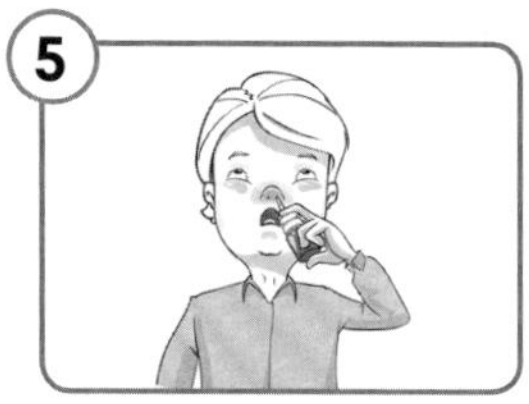

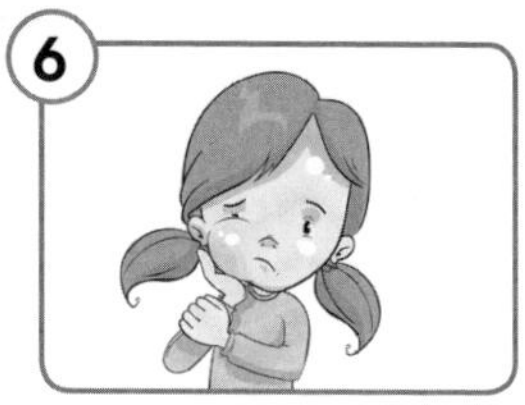

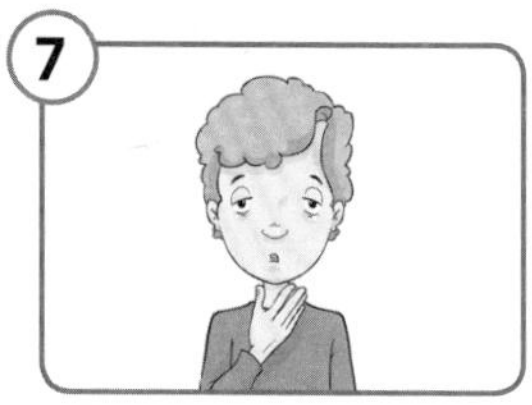

0 Ella has **e**<u>*a r a c h*</u>**e**.

1 Mr White has a bad **c** _ _ **d**. He has a **r** _ _ _ **y** nose and he **s** _ _ _ **zes** a lot.

2 Jessica **c** _ _ _ **hs** a lot.

3 Oscar has a **s** _ _ _ _ _ _ _ _ _ _ **e**.

4 Mrs Jones has a terrible **h** _ _ _ _ _ _ **e** and a **t** _ _ _ _ _ _ _ _ _ **e**.

5 Thomas has a **b** _ _ _ _ _ **d** nose.

6 Betty has **t** _ _ _ _ _ _ _ **e**.

7 Sam has a **s** _ _ **e t** _ _ _ _ **t**.

☐ / 10

---

name ______________________ class ____

5.3 Injuries

A

2 Complete the sentences with the words in the box.

bites ~~broken~~ broken bruise burn cut

0 Andy has got a <u>*broken*</u> arm. He can't write and he can't play tennis.

1 Fred has got a big black and blue __________ on his leg. He bumped into a table.

2 Isabella has lots of red mosquito __________ on her body!

3 Ella fell and now she's got a __________ leg. She can't walk.

4 Sam got a __________ when he was cutting some paper.

5 Millie has a __________ on her hand. She got some very hot water on it.

☐ / 5

---

name ______________________ class ____

5.5 The body

A

3 Match 1–5 to a–e.

0 You eat with these. [*f*]

1 You can't stand without these. They're strong and white. [ ]

2 This is a very important part of your body. It beats all the time. [ ]

3 This is red and it goes all over in your body. [ ]

4 When you exercise, they become bigger and stronger. [ ]

5 This part of your body is in your head. You think with it. [ ]

a blood
b bones
c brain
d heart
e muscles
f teeth

☐ / 5

Your total score ☐ / 20

© Pearson Education Limited 2019 PHOTOCOPIABLE

5 Vocabulary Check B

name ______________________ class ______

5.1 Health problems

B

1 Look at the pictures and complete the sentences.

0 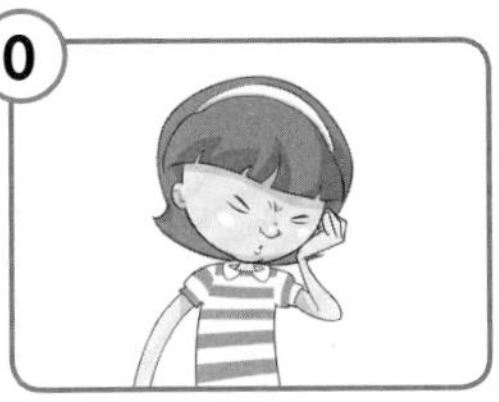

1 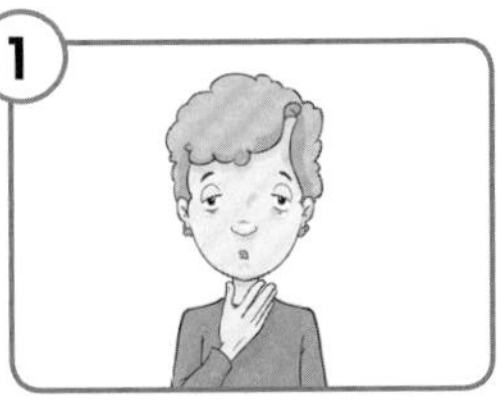

2 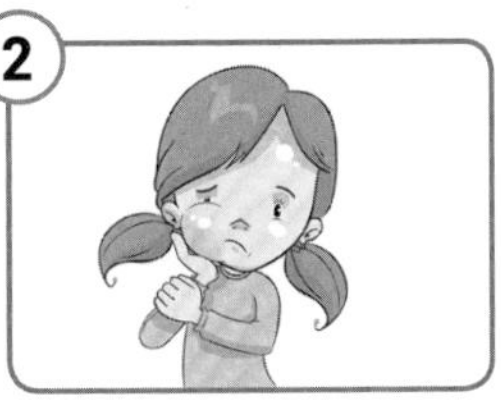

3 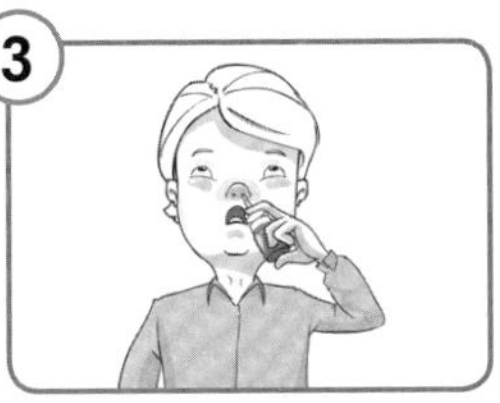

4 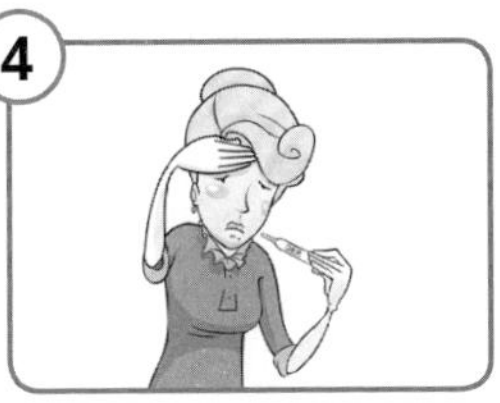

5 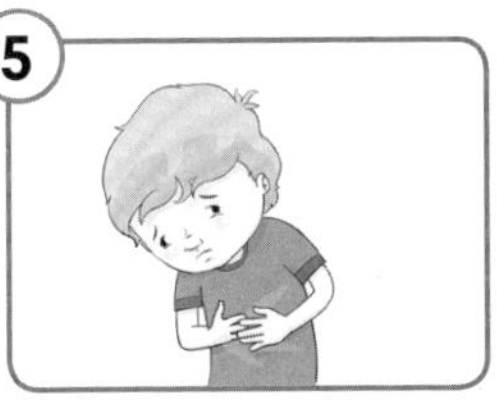

6 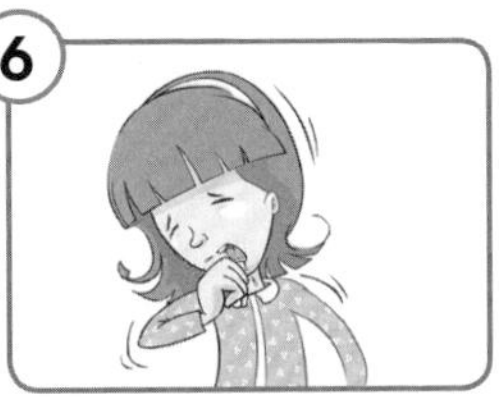

7 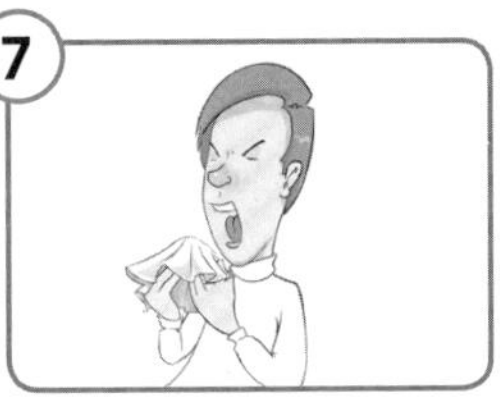

0 Ella has **e**_arach_**e**.
1 Sam has a **s**_ _**e t**_ _ _ _**t**.
2 Betty has **t**_ _ _ _ _ _ _ _**e**.
3 Thomas has a **b**_ _ _ _ _**d** nose.
4 Mrs Jones has a terrible **h**_ _ _ _ _ _**e** and a **t**_ _ _ _ _ _ _ _ _ _**e**.
5 Oscar has a **s**_ _ _ _ _ _ _ _ _ _**e**.
6 Jessica **c**_ _ _**hs** a lot.
7 Mr White has a bad **c**_ _**d**. He has a **r**_ _ _**y** nose and he **s**_ _ _**zes** a lot.

☐ / 10

name ______________________ class ______

5.3 Injuries

B

2 Complete the sentences with the words in the box.

bites ~~broken~~ broken bruise burn cut

0 Andy has got a _broken_ arm. He can't write and he can't play tennis.
1 Neil has a bad __________ on his hand. Some very hot water fell on it.
2 Ricky has red mosquito __________ on his body!
3 Margaret got a __________ on her hand when she was cutting some paper.
4 Stan fell and now he's got a __________ leg. He can't run or walk.
5 Alice has got a black and blue __________ on her leg. She bumped into a table.

☐ / 5

name ______________________ class ______

5.5 The body

B

3 Match 1–5 to a–e.

0 You eat with these. [_f_]
1 You need this to live. It's red and it goes all over in your body. [ ]
2 These are strong and white. You need them to stand. [ ]
3 You think with this part of your body. It is in your head. [ ]
4 When you exercise, they become bigger and stronger. [ ]
5 This beats all the time. It is a very important part of your body. [ ]

a blood
b muscles
c bones
d heart
e brain
f teeth

☐ / 5

Your total score ☐ / 20

© Pearson Education Limited 2019 PHOTOCOPIABLE

6 Vocabulary Check A

______________________________ ____
name class

6.1 Cooking verbs; Cooking nouns

A

1 Look at the pictures and complete the sentences with the words in the box.

bake boil bowl chop oven pan peel pot ~~roast~~ slice tin

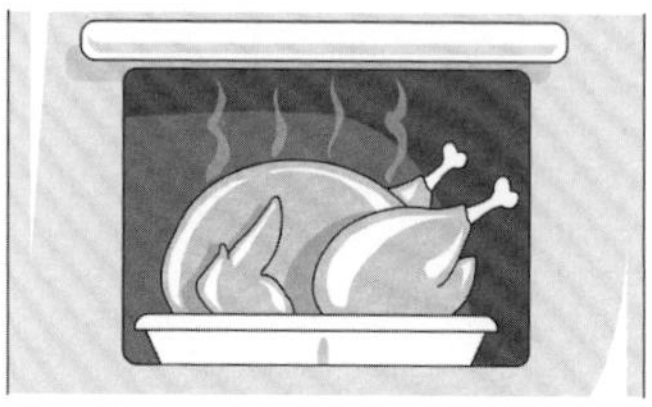

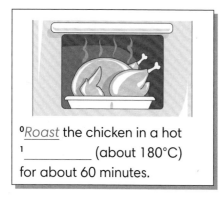

0 *Roast* the chicken in a hot 1 __________ (about 180°C) for about 60 minutes.

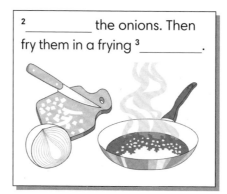

2 __________ the onions. Then fry them in a frying 3 __________.

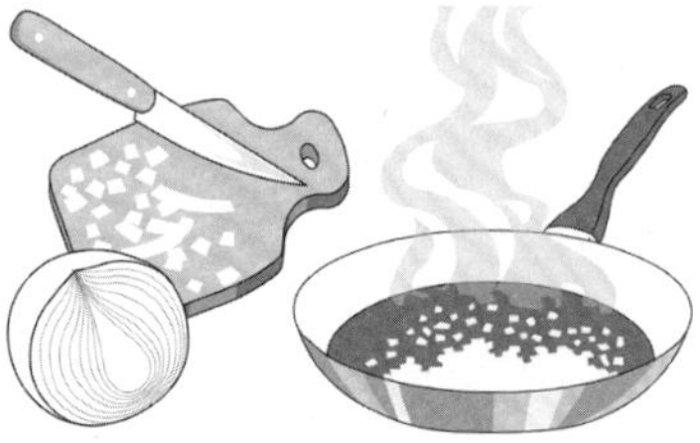

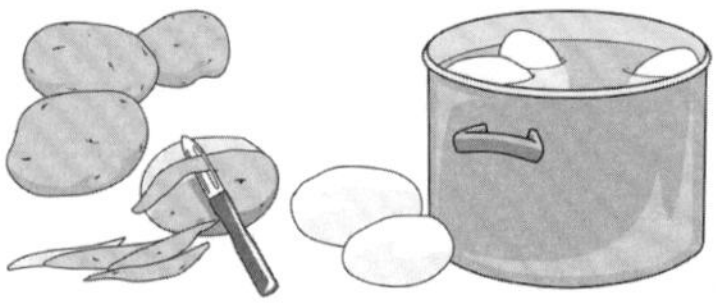

4 __________ the potatoes and put them in a 5 __________. 6 __________ them for ten minutes.

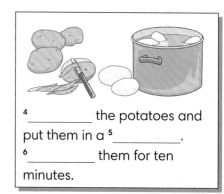

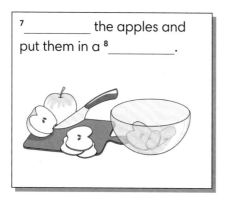

7 __________ the apples and put them in a 8 __________.

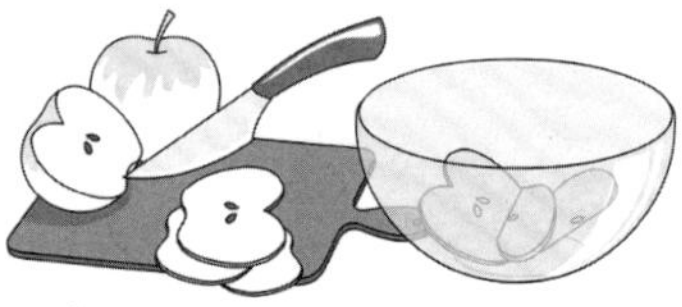

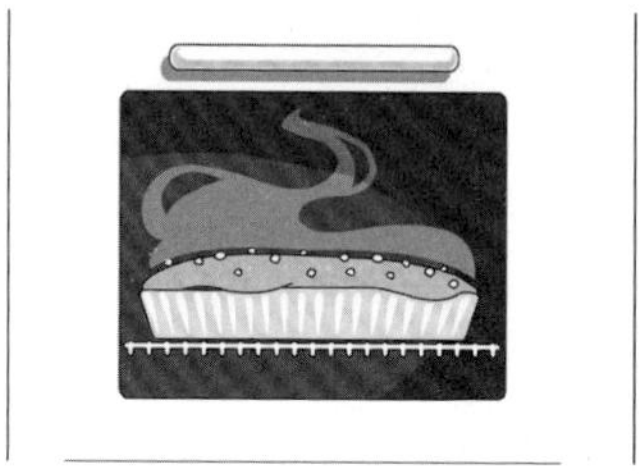

9 __________ the cake in a large round cake 10 __________.

[ ] / [10]

- ✂

______________________________ ____
name class

6.2 Serving and eating food

A

2 Complete the sentences with words for serving and eating food.

0 We put the food on a **p** *l a t e*.
1 We eat soup with a **s**_ _ _ _.
2 We cut bread with a **k**_ _ _ _.
3 We eat pasta with a **f**_ _ _ _.
4 We drink water from a **g**_ _ _ _.
5 We drink coffee from a **c**_ _ _.

[ ] / [5]

- ✂

______________________________ ____
name class

6.5 Describing food

A

3 Circle the correct word.

0 I don't like milk chocolate. It's too [*sweet*] / *spicy*.
1 I love strawberries and cream. They're *delicious* / *disgusting*.
2 Lemons are *sweet* / *sour* but bananas aren't.
3 Are the chips and sausages *salty* / *sweet* enough?
4 Don't eat this! It's *delicious* / *disgusting*.
5 Food with chillies is *sour* / *spicy*.

[ ] / [5]

Your total score [ ] / [20]

© Pearson Education Limited 2019 PHOTOCOPIABLE

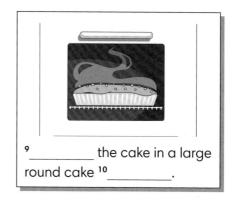

6 Vocabulary Check B

name ______________________ class ______

6.1 Cooking verbs; Cooking nouns

B

1 Look at the pictures and complete the sentences with the words in the box.

bake boil bowl chop oven pan peel pot ~~roast~~ slice tin

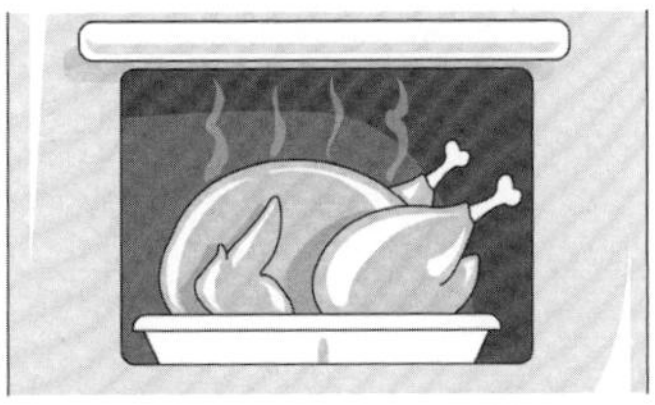

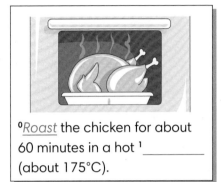

[0] *Roast* the chicken for about 60 minutes in a hot [1] ________ (about 175°C).

[2] ________ the cake in a large round cake [3] ________.

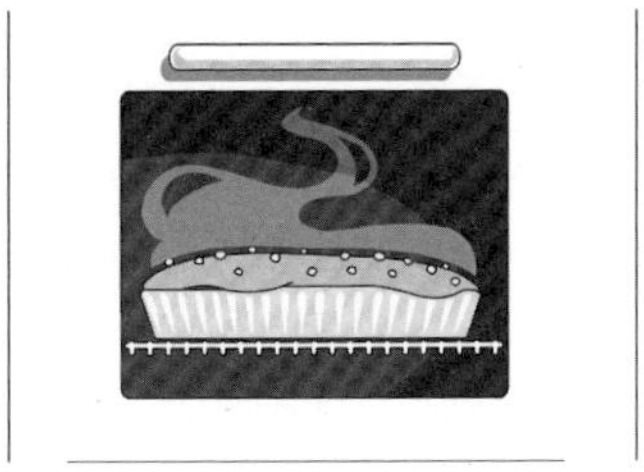

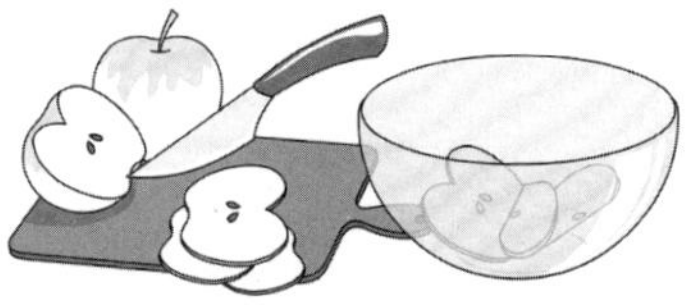

[4] ________ the apples and put them in a [5] ________.

[6] ________ the onions. Then fry them in a frying [7] ________.

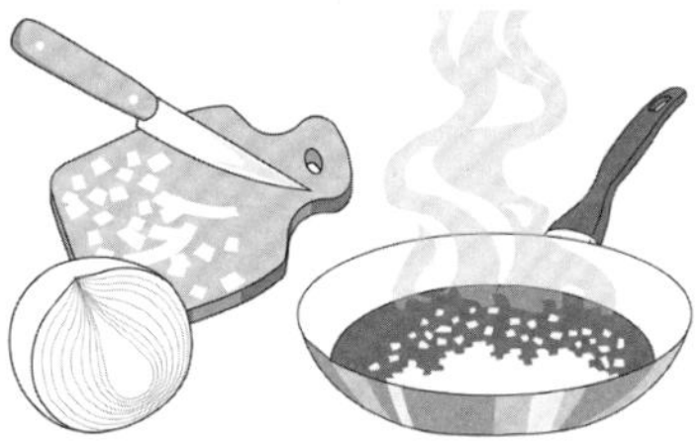

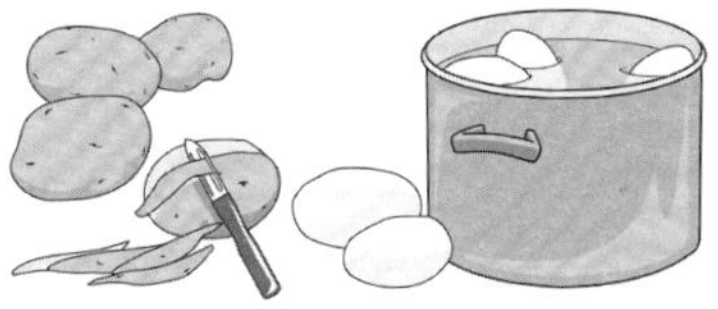

[8] ________ the potatoes and put them in a [9] ________. [10] ________ them for ten minutes.

☐ / 10

name ______________________ class ______

6.2 Serving and eating food

B

2 Complete the sentences with words for serving and eating food.

0 We put the food on a **p** *l a t e*.
1 We eat salad with a **f** _ _ _ _.
2 We drink tea from a **c** _ _.
3 We cut meat with a **k** _ _ _ _.
4 We eat ice cream with a **s** _ _ _ _.
5 We drink juice from a **g** _ _ _ _.

☐ / 5

name ______________________ class ______

6.5 Describing food

B

3 Circle the correct word.

0 I don't like milk chocolate. It's too [sweet] / *spicy*.
1 Don't eat this cheese. It's *disgusting* / *delicious*.
2 There are chillies in this food and it's *sweet* / *spicy*.
3 Lemons are *sour* / *sweet* but bananas aren't.
4 Are the potatoes *disgusting* / *salty* enough?
5 I love Granny's chocolate cake. It's *disgusting* / *delicious*!

☐ / 5

Your total score ☐ / 20

© Pearson Education Limited 2019 PHOTOCOPIABLE

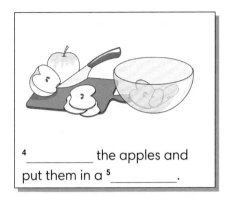

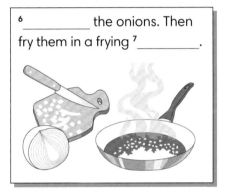

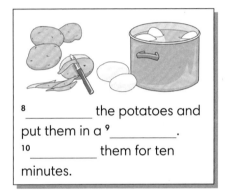

name ______________________ class ______

7.1 Places to live; Parts of the house

A

1 Complete the texts with the words in the box.

attic balcony block ~~city~~ cottage flat lift semi-detached stairs village

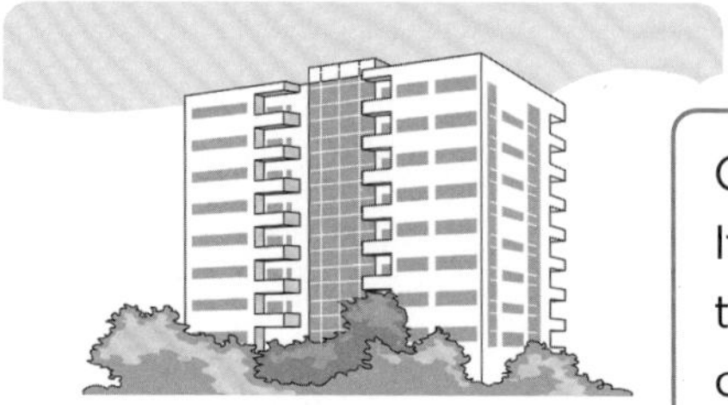

We live in a big [0]*city*. My home is a [1]__________ on the top floor in a [2]__________ of flats. There's a [3]__________ outside my bedroom and the view from there is fantastic. I take the [4]__________ to get to my flat, I don't walk up the stairs.

Our house is an old [5]__________. It's in a small [6]__________ in the country. It's got a garden, a bathroom, a kitchen, a living room and two bedrooms. My bedroom is in the [7]__________ at the top of the house.

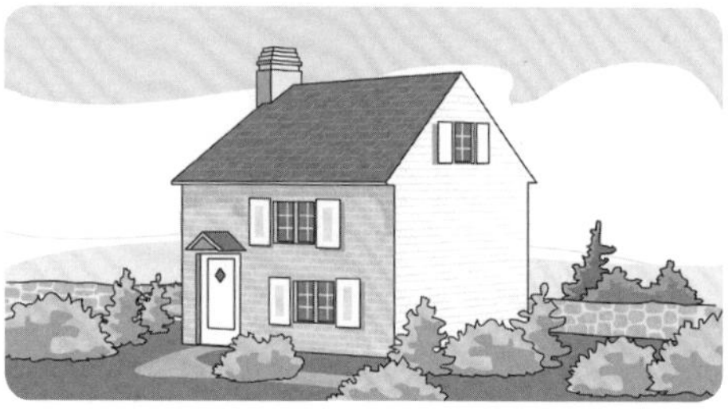

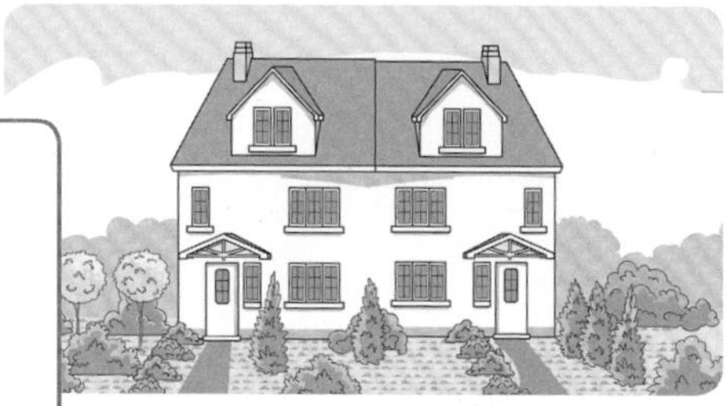

Our home is a [8]__________ house. It's in a small town in Scotland. Our living room is next to our neighbour's living room and we can hear their TV every night. My room is in the attic and I have to walk up many [9]__________.

[ ] / 9

name ______________________ class ______

7.3 In the house

A

2 Complete the sentences.

0 I sit at my **d** *e s k* to do my homework.
1 Hot water comes out of that **t** _ _.
2 I always check my face in the **m** _ _ _ _ _ before I go out.
3 I wash the dishes in the kitchen **s** _ _ _.
4 My pens are in a **d** _ _ _ _ _ in my desk.
5 The plates and bowls are in a kitchen **c** _ _ _ _ _ _ _.
6 All my books are in the **b** _ _ _ _ _ _ _ _.

[ ] / 6

name ______________________ class ______

7.5 Phrasal verbs

A

3 Complete the sentences with *for*, *out* or *up*.

0 Get *up*! It's very late.
1 Check __________ this new sports website. It looks interesting.
2 I want to find __________ more about garden birds.
3 In summer I wake __________ early and go to bed late.
4 Let's look __________ some new games on the Internet.
5 When you finish cooking, please clean __________ the kitchen.

[ ] / 5

Your total score [ ] / 20

© Pearson Education Limited 2019 PHOTOCOPIABLE

7 Vocabulary Check B

name ______________________ class ________

7.1 Places to live; Parts of the house

B

1 Complete the texts with the words in the box.

attic balcony block ~~city~~ cottage floor lift semi-detached stairs village

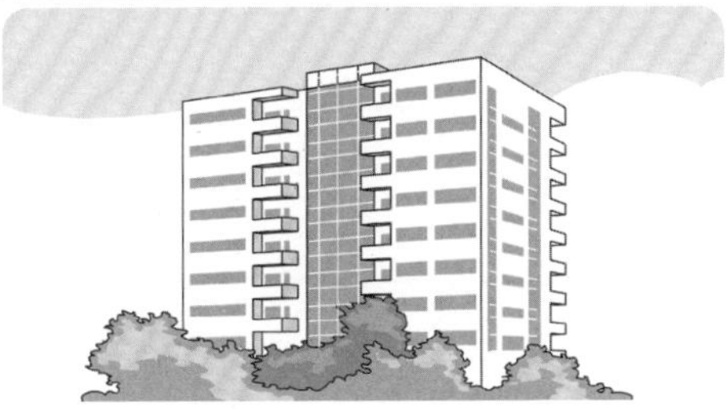

I live in London – it's a very big [0] *city*. Our flat is in a big [1] __________ of flats. We always use the [2] __________ to get to our flat because it's on the eleventh [3] __________. There's a [4] __________ outside the living room and the view from there is fantastic.

I live in a town in England. Our home is a [5] __________ house. Our living room is next to our neighbour's living room and we can hear their TV at night. I have to walk up and down [6] __________ because my bedroom is in the [7] __________.

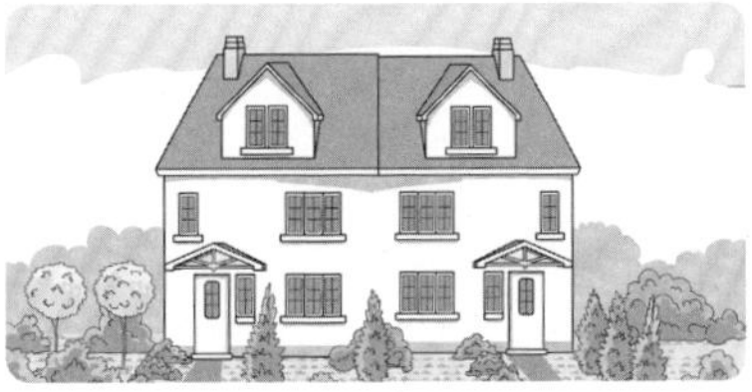

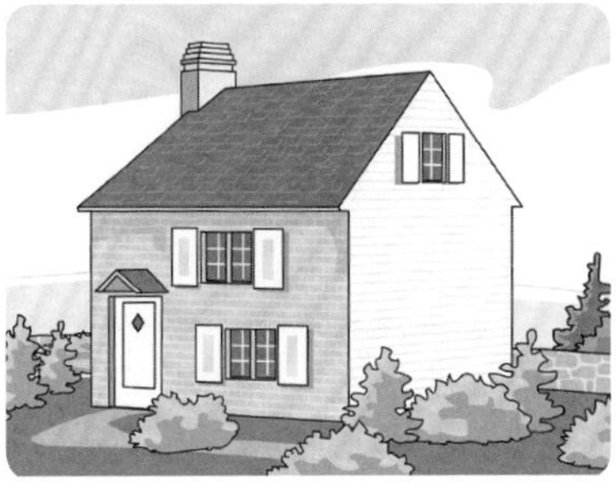

Our home is an old [8] __________. It's in a small [9] __________ in the country. It's got a garden, a kitchen, a living room, a bathroom and two bedrooms.

☐ / 9

name ______________________ class ________

7.3 In the house

B

2 Complete the sentences.

0 I sit at my **d** *e s k* to do my homework.

1 All my books are in the **b** _ _ _ _ _ _ _ _.

2 The cups and mugs are in that **c** _ _ _ _ _ _ _.

3 She washes the glasses in the kitchen **s** _ _ _, not a dishwasher.

4 Cold water comes out of this **t** _ _.

5 He always checks his clothes in the **m** _ _ _ _ _ before he leaves the house.

6 There's some paper in the **d** _ _ _ _ _ in my desk.

☐ / 6

name ______________________ class ________

7.5 Phrasal verbs

B

3 Complete the sentences with *for*, *out* or *up*.

0 Get *up*! It's very late.

1 Please clean __________ when you finish painting the room.

2 When they are on holiday, they wake __________ early and go to bed late.

3 Check __________ these photos. They're fantastic!

4 Please help me look __________ my keys.

5 Do you want to find __________ more about the history of the UK?

☐ / 5

Your total score ☐ / 20

© Pearson Education Limited 2019 PHOTOCOPIABLE

8 Vocabulary Check A

name ______________________ class ______

8.1 Life ambitions

A

1 Complete the texts. Use *be*, *have*, *learn* and *live*.

I want to [0] *be* a writer. I hope my books are popular because I'd love to [1] __________ famous! My other ambition is to [2] __________ foreign languages – Spanish and French. I want to [3] __________ abroad.

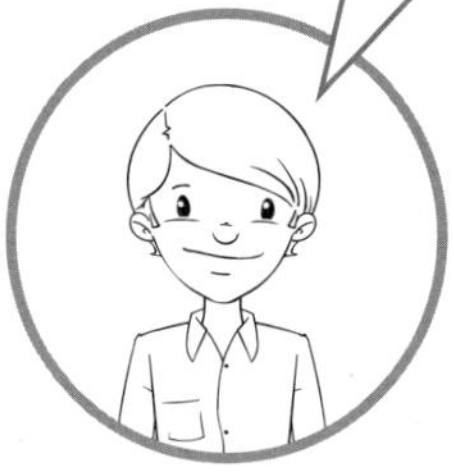

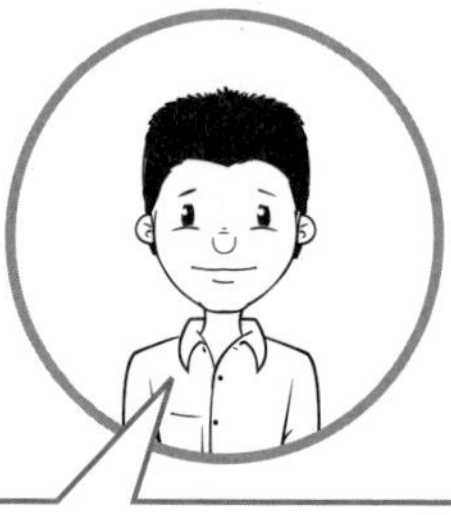

I'd love to [4] __________ my own business. I also want to [5] __________ rich and have a house with a garden. I want to [6] __________ a family with four children!

My ambition is to [7] __________ to paint well. I don't want to [8] __________ an artist, but it's important to [9] __________ an interesting hobby. I want to [10] __________ on my own in a big city.

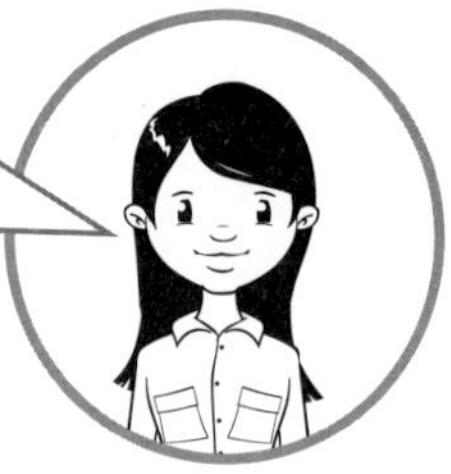

[ ] / [10]

name ______________________ class ______

8.3 Being with people

A

2 Complete the sentences with the words in the box.

~~call~~ give invite kiss shake visit

0 Don't forget to *call* your granny on her birthday.
1 My grandparents always __________ me a hug when I visit them.
2 He is going to __________ all his friends to his party.
3 We should __________ friends in hospital.
4 It's polite to __________ hands when you meet a person for the first time.
5 When I leave home, I __________ my mum and dad goodbye.

[ ] / [5]

name ______________________ class ______

8.5 Good manners

A

3 Complete the text.

Good manners are important!

0 Be *polite* to everyone.
1 You should always arrive **o**__________ time.
2 Don't be **l**__________ for meetings.
3 Ask for **p**__________ before you borrow someone's things.
4 Be patient and wait your **t**__________.
5 Don't **i**__________. Wait for other people to finish talking.

[ ] / [5]

Your total score [ ] / [20]

© Pearson Education Limited 2019 PHOTOCOPIABLE

8 Vocabulary Check B

name ______________________ class ________

8.1 Life ambitions

B

1 Complete the texts. Use *be*, *have*, *learn* and *live*.

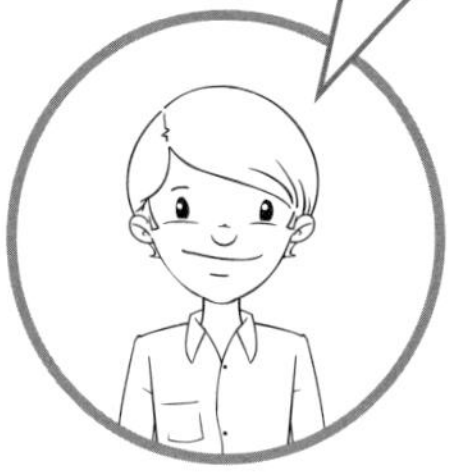

I want to [0] *be* an actor because I'd love to [1] ________ famous. I want to [2] ________ on my own. My other ambition is to [3] ________ foreign languages and travel around the world.

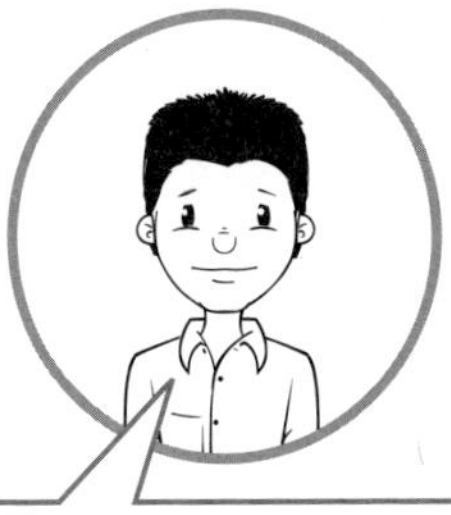

I want to [4] ________ a family with four children! My other ambition is to [5] ________ to paint very well. I don't want to [6] ________ an artist, but it's important to [7] ________ a hobby.

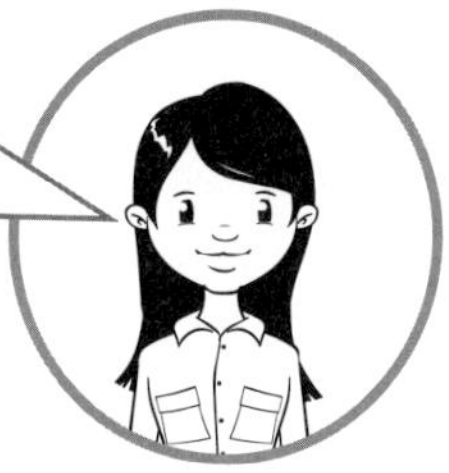

I'd love to [8] ________ my own business. I want to [9] ________ rich, have a big house and go on expensive holidays. I also want to [10] ________ abroad in a warm country.

☐ / 10

name ______________________ class ________

8.3 Being with people

B

2 Complete the sentences with the words in the box.

~~call~~ give invite kiss shake visit

0 Don't forget to *call* your granny on her birthday.
1 When you meet a person for the first time, smile and ________ hands.
2 I always ________ my mum a hug before I go to school.
3 Please come and ________ me in Scotland in the summer.
4 I'm going to ________ all my school friends to my party.
5 Do you ________ your friends when you meet them?

☐ / 5

name ______________________ class ________

8.5 Good manners

B

3 Complete the text.

Good manners are important!

0 Always be *polite* to everyone.
1 Don't be **l**________ for meetings.
2 You must always arrive **o**________ time.
3 Wait your **t**________ and be patient.
4 Wait for other people to finish talking. Don't **i**________.
5 When you want to borrow something, always ask for **p**________.

☐ / 5

Your total score ☐ / 20

© Pearson Education Limited 2019 PHOTOCOPIABLE

1 Grammar Check A

name ______________________ class ______

1.2 Present Continuous — A

1 Complete the text with the Present Continuous form of the verbs.

It's Saturday morning. We [0] *are helping* (help) Dad with the chores. Mum [1] ______________ (not do) any chores today, because she's at work. I [2] ______________ (vacuum) the living room and my sister [3] ______________ (iron) the clothes. My little brothers [4] ______________ (make) their beds. And where is Dad? [5] ______________ (he / load) the washing machine?

☐ / 5

1.2 Stative verbs — A

2 Complete the sentences with the Present Simple or the Present Continuous form of the verbs.

0 I *like* (like) this book. It's interesting.
1 The boy ______________ (want) to play his new computer game now.
2 Can you help me? I ______________ (not understand) this exercise.
3 ______________ (you / know) the answer to this question?
4 I ______________ (make) a cake right now and I ______________ (need) some help.

☐ / 5

name ______________________ class ______

1.3 Present Simple and Present Continuous — A

3 Circle the correct answer.

0 I (clear) / *'m clearing* the table after breakfast every day.
1 Mark *wears / is wearing* his favourite T-shirt today.
2 We *don't go / aren't going* to school on Saturdays.
3 *Does Gran sleep / Is Gran sleeping* at the moment?
4 I *tidy / 'm tidying* my room every weekend.
5 Dad *takes / is taking* out the rubbish right now.

☐ / 5

Your total score ☐ / 15

1 Grammar Check B

name ______________________ class ______

1.2 Present Continuous — B

1 Complete the text with the Present Continuous form of the verbs.

It's Saturday morning. We [0] *are helping* (help) Mum with the chores. Dad is at work, so he [1] ______________ (not do) any chores today. Mum [2] ______________ (cook) in the kitchen. I [3] ______________ (water) the plants and my sisters [4] ______________ (hang) out the washing. But where is my little brother? [5] ______________ (he / take) out the rubbish?

☐ / 5

1.2 Stative verbs — B

2 Complete the sentences with the Present Simple or the Present Continuous form of the verbs.

0 I *like* (like) this book. It's interesting.
1 Dad, are you busy right now? I ______________ (need) some help.
2 Mum ______________ (want) to watch the tennis match on TV now.
3 I ______________ (do) my homework now and I ______________ (not understand) this exercise.
4 ______________ (you / know) the answer to this question?

☐ / 5

name ______________________ class ______

1.3 Present Simple and Present Continuous — B

3 Circle the correct answer.

0 I (clear) / *'m clearing* the table after breakfast every day.
1 *Does Mum work / Is Mum working* at the moment?
2 I *load / 'm loading* the washing machine right now.
3 Ann *tidies / is tidying* her room every weekend.
4 Dad *wears / is wearing* a funny hat today.
5 We *don't go / aren't going* to the cinema on Mondays.

☐ / 5

Your total score ☐ / 15

© Pearson Education Limited 2019 PHOTOCOPIABLE

name   class

name   class

2.2 Comparative and superlative A adjectives

1 **Complete the sentences with the comparative or superlative form of the adjectives.**

0 Shopping is _the most boring_ (boring) activity in the world!

1 Who is _____ (fast) runner in the team?

2 This is _____ (big) cinema in our town.

3 Judy is a _____ (good) dancer than her brother.

4 This bag is _____ (expensive) one in the shop.

5 Mum is _____ (organised) than Dad.

6 Sue is _____ (sporty) than Tom.

7 You aren't good at music, but I'm _____ (bad) than you.

◯ / ⑦

2.2 Comparative and superlative B adjectives

1 **Complete the sentences with the comparative or superlative form of the adjectives.**

0 Shopping is _the most boring_ (boring) activity in the world!

1 Sam is _____ (sporty) boy in our class.

2 Dad's bike is _____ (big) than my bike.

3 Today is _____ (good) day of my life.

4 Jim is a _____ (fast) runner than Tom.

5 My sister isn't good at cooking, but I'm _____ (bad) than her!

6 This bag is _____ (expensive) than that one.

7 Grandad is _____ (organised) person in my family.

◯ / ⑦

name   class

name   class

2.3 too, not … enough, (not) as … as A

2 **Complete the sentences with too or enough.**

0 This T-shirt is too small for me.
This T-shirt isn't _big enough_ for me. (big)

1 The blue dress isn't cheap enough.
The blue dress is _____. (expensive)

2 These jeans are too dirty.
These jeans aren't _____. (clean)

3 Jim can't drive a car. He isn't old enough.
He's _____. (young)

4 This game is too boring.
This game isn't _____. (interesting)

◯ / ④

3 **Complete the sentences with is/isn't as … as.**

0 Jack is younger than Meg.
Jack _isn't as_ old _as_ Meg.

1 Meg and Jack are short.
Meg _____ short _____ Jack.

2 Jack and Meg are intelligent.
Jack _____ intelligent _____ Meg.

3 Meg is messier than Jack.
Jack _____ messy _____ Meg.

4 Jack is stronger than Meg.
Meg _____ strong _____ Jack.

◯ / ④

Your total score ◯ / ⑮

2.3 too, not … enough, (not) as … as B

2 **Complete the sentences with too or enough.**

0 This T-shirt is too small for me.
This T-shirt isn't _big enough_ for me. (big)

1 These shoes aren't clean enough.
These shoes are _____. (dirty)

2 This sofa is too expensive.
This sofa isn't _____. (cheap)

3 The film isn't interesting enough.
The film is _____. (boring)

4 Ann can't drive a car. She's too young.
She isn't _____. (old)

◯ / ④

3 **Complete the sentences with is/isn't as … as.**

0 Amy is younger than Mike.
Amy _isn't as_ old _as_ Mike.

1 Amy and Mike are intelligent.
Amy _____ intelligent _____ Mike.

2 Mike is tidier than Amy.
Amy _____ tidy _____ Mike.

3 Mike and Amy are tall.
Mike _____ tall _____ Amy.

4 Amy is faster than Mike.
Mike _____ fast _____ Amy.

◯ / ④

Your total score ◯ / ⑮

© Pearson Education Limited 2019   PHOTOCOPIABLE

name _____ class _____

3.2 Past Simple affirmative and negative **A**

1 Complete the email with the Past Simple form of the verbs in brackets.

Hi Mark,

How are you?

My family and I ⁰*were* (be) on holiday in Spain last month. We ¹_____ (not go) there by plane – we ²_____ (take) the train. We ³_____ (visit) some interesting museums and I ⁴_____ (swim) in the sea every day. In the evenings, we ⁵_____ (not have) dinner at the hotel. We ⁶_____ (go) to small Spanish restaurants. The local food ⁷_____ (be) fantastic.

See you soon.

Lisa

☐ / ⑦

---

name _____ class _____

3.3 Past Simple questions and short answers **A**

2 Complete the questions with the Past Simple form of the verbs. Then complete the short answers.

0 **A:** *Did you see* (you / see) the Eiffel Tower in Paris?

　B: Yes, *I did*.

1 **A:** _____
(the weather / be) good yesterday?

　B: Yes, _____.

2 **A:** _____
(Emily / take) any photos?

　B: No, _____.

3 **A:** _____
(Jake and Kim / be) on time for the bus?

　B: No, _____.

4 **A:** _____
(you and Sam / go) to the beach?

　B: Yes, _____.

☐ / ⑧

Your total score ☐ / ⑮

---

nname _____ class _____

3.2 Past Simple affirmative and negative **B**

1 Complete the email with the Past Simple form of the verbs in brackets.

Hi Lisa,

How are you?

My family and I ⁰*were* (be) on holiday in Italy last month. We ¹_____ (go) there by plane – we ²_____ (not take) the train. My sister and I ³_____ (swim) in the sea every day. We ⁴_____ (visit) some museums too. In the evenings, we ⁵_____ (not stay) in our hotel. We ⁶_____ (have) dinner in small Italian restaurants. The food ⁷_____ (be) fantastic.

See you soon.

Matt

☐ / ⑦

---

name _____ class _____

3.3 Past Simple questions and short answers **B**

2 Complete the questions with the Past Simple form of the verbs. Then complete the short answers.

0 **A:** *Did you see* (you / see) the Eiffel Tower in Paris?

　B: Yes, *I did*.

1 **A:** _____
(you and Jim / be) tired after the trip?

　B: No, _____.

2 **A:** _____
(Liz and Kevin / explore) the town?

　B: Yes, _____.

3 **A:** _____
(Fred / forget) his camera?

　B: No, _____.

4 **A:** _____
(the weather / be) cold yesterday?

　B: Yes, _____.

☐ / ⑧

Your total score ☐ / ⑮

© Pearson Education Limited 2019　PHOTOCOPIABLE

4 Grammar Check A

name ______ class ______

4.2 Past Continuous A

1 Complete the sentences with the Past Continuous form of the verbs.

0 My friends and I *were hanging out* (hang out) in the park at one o'clock.
1 Adam ______ (play) football ten minutes ago.
2 They ______ (not watch) TV at two o'clock.
3 What ______ (you / do) yesterday at five o'clock?
4 Anna ______ (not surf) the Internet an hour ago.
5 ______ Jim ______ (look) for the remote control a minute ago?

[ ] / [5]

name ______ class ______

4.3 Past Continuous and Past Simple with *when* A

2 Circle the correct answer.

0 I *dried* / *was drying* my hair when you *phoned* / *were phoning* me.
1 We *used* / *were using* the toaster when the bread *fell* / *was falling* on the floor.
2 They *shopped* / *were shopping* for a hairdryer when I *saw* / *was seeing* them.
3 *Did she have* / *Was she having* a shower when the postman *arrived* / *was arriving*?

[ ] / [6]

4.3 Adverbs of manner

3 Complete the sentences with adverbs of manner.

0 Please do your work *carefully*. (careful)
1 The children played together ______. (happy)
2 He walked out of the room ______. (quiet)
3 You can sing very ______. (good)
4 She played the guitar ______. (loud)

[ ] / [4]

Your total score [ ] / [15]

4 Grammar Check B

name ______ class ______

4.2 Past Continuous B

1 Complete the sentences with the Past Continuous form of the verbs.

0 My friends and I *were hanging out* (hang out) in the park at one o'clock.
1 What ______ (they / do) at six o'clock yesterday?
2 Dave ______ (not watch) a film an hour ago.
3 At five o'clock, I ______ (study) in the library.
4 ______ Anna ______ (use) the blender ten minutes ago?
5 Jim and Sam ______ (not play) basketball five minutes ago.

[ ] / [5]

name ______ class ______

4.3 Past Continuous and Past Simple with *when* B

2 Circle the correct answer.

0 I *dried* / *was drying* my hair when you *phoned* / *were phoning* me.
1 *Did he surf* / *Was he surfing* the Internet when the storm *started* / *was starting*?
2 We *had* / *were having* dinner when Aunt Mary *arrived* / *was arriving*.
3 They *bought* / *were buying* a smart TV when I *saw* / *was seeing* them.

[ ] / [6]

4.3 Adverbs of manner

3 Complete the sentences with adverbs of manner.

0 Please do your work *carefully*. (careful)
1 You play the guitar very ______. (good)
2 The children did the exercises ______. (easy)
3 The baby is sleeping. Please talk ______. (quiet)
4 He sang the song ______. (loud)

[ ] / [4]

Your total score [ ] / [15]

© Pearson Education Limited 2019 PHOTOCOPIABLE

5 Grammar Check A

name ______ class ______

5.2 *have to* A

1 Complete the sentences with the correct form of *have to* and the verbs in brackets.

0 I'm very ill. I *have to see* (see) the doctor. (✓)
1 Relax! You ______ (work) so hard. (✗)
2 Jim has a music exam next week. He ______ (practise) the piano. (✓)
3 Meg has got a runny nose, but she ______ (stay) in bed. (✗)
4 I ______ (help) my parents with the housework. (✓)
5 The children ______ (go) to bed early on Saturdays. (✗)

☐ / [5]

2 Complete the questions with the correct form of *have to*.

0 *Does* Dad *have to* work so hard?
1 When ______ we ______ be back home?
2 ______ Jack ______ get up early in the morning?'
3 What ______ she ______ do now?
4 ______ they ______ study for the test today?

☐ / [4]

name ______ class ______

5.3 *should* A

2 Circle the correct answer.

Lily: Hey, Joe. You don't look very well.
Joe: I feel ill.
Lily: You [0] *should* / *(shouldn't)* be at school.
Joe: But we have a test today.
Lily: I think you [1] *should* / *shouldn't* tell the teacher.
Joe: I think I've got a temperature too. What [2] *I should* / *should I* do?
Lily: You [3] *should* / *shouldn't* call your parents.
Joe: Ok. [4] *Should I* / *I should* wait for them outside?
Lily: No, you [5] *should* / *shouldn't*. Let's wait for them in the school office.
Joe: Good idea.

☐ / [6]

Your total score ☐ / [15]

5 Grammar Check B

name ______ class ______

5.2 *have to* B

1 Complete the sentences with the correct form of *have to* and the verbs in brackets.

0 I'm very ill. I *have to see* (see) the doctor. (✓)
1 Luke ______ (help) his parents with the chores. (✓)
2 You can do it later. You ______ (do) it now. (✗)
3 We have a music exam tomorrow. We ______ (practise) the guitar. (✓)
4 It's a holiday. They ______ (work) today. (✗)
5 Dave isn't ill. He ______ (stay) in bed. (✗)

☐ / [5]

2 Complete the questions with the correct form of *have to*.

0 *Does* Dad *have to* work so hard?
1 ______ we ______ go to bed early today?
2 What ______ he ______ do now?
3 ______ Maria ______ get up early in the morning?'
4 When ______ they ______ be back home?

☐ / [4]

name ______ class ______

5.3 *should* B

2 Circle the correct answer.

Kate: Hey, Paul. What's wrong?
Paul: I feel ill and I've got a temperature.
Kate: You [0] *(should)* / *shouldn't* go home.
Paul: But I have a guitar lesson this afternoon.
Kate: You [1] *should* / *shouldn't* tell your teacher you're ill. You [2] *should* / *shouldn't* be with other people.
Paul: [3] *I should* / *Should I* see the doctor?
Kate: Yes, you [4] *should* / *shouldn't*.
Paul: What [5] *I should* / *should I* do?
Kate: Let's go to the school office and call your parents.
Paul: Good idea.

☐ / [6]

Your total score ☐ / [15]

PHOTOCOPIABLE © Pearson Education Limited 2019

_____
name   class

6.2 Present Perfect affirmative and negative   **A**

1 Complete the sentences with the Present Perfect form of the verbs.

0 Mum *has baked* (bake) a carrot cake for dessert.

1 Kate _____ (leave) some cake for you in the fridge.

2 I _____ (not chop) the vegetables, but I _____ (wash) them.

3 Bruno _____ (not eat) his food. Is he ill?

4 They _____ (have) dinner, so they aren't hungry.

5 We _____ (make) lemonade. Would you like some?

6 Dad _____ (not tidy) the kitchen and it's a mess!

☐ / ⑦

_____
name   class

6.3 Present Perfect questions, *ever*, *never*   **A**

2 Complete the Present Perfect questions and answers.

0 A: *Have you ever cooked* (you / ever / cook) pasta?
   B: Yes, I *have*.

1 A: _____
     (Ted / ever / try) Mexican food?
   B: No, _____
     (he / never / try) it.

2 A: _____ (they / win) the competition?
   B: Yes, they _____.

3 A: _____
     (your sister / ever / make) biscuits?
   B: No, _____
     (she / never / make) biscuits.

4 A: _____
     (you / ever / have) the flu?
   B: No, I _____. I'm very healthy.

☐ / ⑧

Your total score ☐ / ⑮

_____
name   class

6.2 Present Perfect affirmative and negative   **B**

1 Complete the sentences with the Present Perfect form of the verbs.

0 Mum *has baked* (bake) a carrot cake for dessert.

1 Daisy _____ (eat) all the biscuits.

2 We _____ (make) some sandwiches. Would you like one?

3 Are you thirsty? I _____ (leave) some lemonade for you.

4 They _____ (not tidy) their bedrooms and they're a mess!

5 The boy _____ (not have) dinner, so he's very hungry.

6 I _____ (wash) the apples, but I _____ (not slice) them.

☐ / ⑦

_____
name   class

6.3 Present Perfect questions, *ever*, *never*   **B**

2 Complete the Present Perfect questions and answers.

0 A: *Have you ever cooked* (you / ever / cook) pasta?
   B: Yes, I *have*.

1 A: _____ (you / have) dinner?
   B: No, I _____. I'm very hungry!

2 A: _____
     (Tess / ever / hear) this song?
   B: No, _____
     (she / never / heard) it.

3 A: _____
     (they / ever / work) together?
   B: No, _____
     (they / never / work) together.

4 A: _____
     (she / ever / win) a competition?
   B: Yes, she _____.

☐ / ⑧

Your total score ☐ / ⑮

© Pearson Education Limited 2019

PHOTOCOPIABLE

name _____ class _____

7.2 Present Continuous for future arrangements   A

1 Complete the dialogues with the Present Continuous form of the verbs.

Luke: Hi, Katy. I ⁰*'m meeting* (meet) Gill after school. We ¹_____ (study) together at her house this afternoon. ² _____ (you / come) too?

Katy: No, sorry. Dad ³_____ (pick) me up in five minutes. I ⁴_____ (go) to my music lesson at three.

- -

Izzie: When ⁵_____ (your parents / fly) to London?

Neil: Tomorrow, but they ⁶_____ (not stay) there long – only two days.

Izzie: Well, I ⁷_____ (not go) anywhere tomorrow. Do you want to hang out?

Neil: Yes, that sounds good.

☐ / ⑦

name _____ class _____

7.3 *must, mustn't, can*   A

2 Complete the texts with *must, mustn't* or *can*.

> **To all students!**
> ✔ Don't forget! The concert is at 7 o'clock on Friday.
> ✔ You ⁰*must* all be here ten minutes before the concert.
> ✔ You ¹_____ forget to turn off your mobile phones.
> ✔ You ²_____ eat during the break, but not when people are performing.

> **Visitors:** You ³_____ take photos in the museum, but only in some rooms.
> You ⁴_____ eat or drink in the museum. You can visit the café next door.
> You ⁵_____ leave the museum before it closes at six o'clock.

> Hi Clare!
> Thanks for looking after the children tonight. You ⁶_____ use my computer — I don't mind. You ⁷_____ let the children stay up after 9 p.m. because they have school tomorrow. Don't forget — you ⁸_____ lock the door before it gets dark.
> See you tomorrow.
> Karen

☐ / ⑧

Your total score ☐ / ⑮

name _____ class _____

7.2 Present Continuous for future arrangements   B

1 Complete the dialogues with the Present Continuous form of the verbs.

Kevin: Hi, Anne. I ⁰*'m meeting* (meet) Wendy at five o'clock. We ¹_____ (play) games at her house this afternoon. ² _____ (you / come)?

Anne: No, sorry. I ³_____ (go) to the dentist's. Mum ⁴_____ (pick) me up in five minutes.

- -

Lily: What time ⁵_____ (your cousins / arrive) tonight?

Rick: I'm not sure. They ⁶_____ (not take) the train, so they may be late.

Lily: Well, I ⁷_____ (not do) anything today. Do you want to hang out?

Rick: Yes, that sounds good.

☐ / ⑦

name _____ class _____

7.3 *must, mustn't, can*   B

2 Complete the texts with *must, mustn't* or *can*.

> **To all students!**
> ✔ Don't forget! The concert is at 7 o'clock on Friday.
> ✔ You ⁰*must* all be here ten minutes before the concert.
> ✔ You ¹_____ have a snack in the interval, but not during the performance.
> ✔ You ²_____ forget to turn off your mobile phones.

> Hi Don!
> Thanks for looking after the house tonight. Remember: you ³_____ lock the door before it gets dark. You ⁴_____ let the cats in the kitchen because they climb on the tables. You ⁵_____ use my computer — I don't mind.
> See you tomorrow.
> Barbara

> **Visitors:** You ⁶_____ eat or drink in the museum. You can visit the café next door.
> You ⁷_____ take photos, but only in some rooms.
> You ⁸_____ leave the museum before it closes at six o'clock.

☐ / ⑧

Your total score ☐ / ⑮

© Pearson Education Limited 2019   PHOTOCOPIABLE

name   class

8.2 *will* for predictions   A

1 Complete the sentences with the correct form of *will*. Use the short form where possible.

0 When I'm older, I'*ll travel* (travel) all around the world.

1 I'm sure you _____ (pass) your exams.

2 Maybe we _____ (not be) rich in the future, but we _____ (be) happy.

3 _____ (you / go) to China next year?

4 Mary _____ (have) a big family one day. She loves children.

5 _____ (she / enjoy) her trip abroad next summer?

6 When _____ (they / buy) a new car?

7 I _____ (not live) in a big city in the future.

☐ / 8

name   class

8.3 Questions and question words   A

2 Read the answers and complete the questions. Write one word in each gap.

0 A: Who *called* you last night?
 B: Ellie called me.

1 A: _____ do you like doing in your free time?
 B: I like playing football.

2 A: Where _____ they live in the future?
 B: They'll live abroad.

3 A: _____ is Freddie sleeping?
 B: Freddie is sleeping because he's tired.

4 A: How often _____ she meet her friends in town?
 B: She meets them twice a week.

5 A: When _____ you see the film?
 B: We saw it last night.

6 A: What _____ they doing yesterday at 5 o'clock?
 B: They were helping their parents.

7 A: Who _____ she going to invite to her party?
 B: She's going to invite all her friends.

☐ / 7

name   class

8.2 *will* for predictions   B

1 Complete the sentences with the correct form of *will*. Use the short form where possible.

0 When I'm older, I'*ll travel* (travel) all around the world.

1 Mike wants to have an interesting job, but he _____ (not have) his own business.

2 When _____ (they / buy) a house?

3 I'm sure she _____ (pass) her exams.

4 _____ (you / enjoy) your trip abroad next June?

5 Marcus _____ (not live) in a big city when he's older.

6 We _____ (not be) famous in the future, but I'm sure we _____ (be) happy.

7 _____ (she / go) to Italy one day?

☐ / 8

name   class

8.3 Questions and question words   B

2 Read the answers and complete the questions. Write one word in each gap.

0 A: Who *called* you last night?
 B: Ellie called me.

1 A: _____ is Alison going home?
 B: She's going home because she's tired.

2 A: When _____ you meet Brian?
 B: I met him last night.

3 A: What _____ he going to make for lunch?
 B: He's going to make spaghetti.

4 A: What _____ you doing yesterday at 3 o'clock?
 B: We were hanging out with our friends.

5 A: How often _____ she brush her teeth?
 B: She brushes them twice a day.

6 A: Where _____ they study in the future?
 B: They'll study abroad.

7 A: _____ do you like doing in your free time?
 B: I like watching films.

☐ / 7

© Pearson Education Limited 2019   PHOTOCOPIABLE

name ______________________ class ________

Vocabulary

1 Look at the pictures and complete the text.

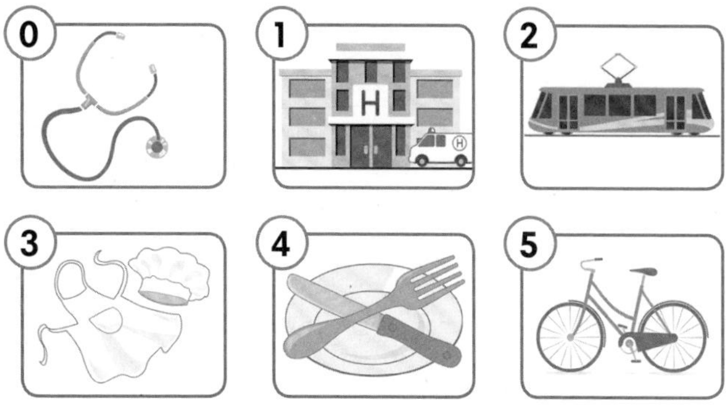

My mum is a [0] d*octor*. She works in a [1] h__________ in the centre of town. She goes to work by [2] t__________. Dad is a [3] c__________. He works in a famous [4] r__________. He doesn't like taking the bus, so he rides his [5] b__________ to work.

__ / 5

2 Circle the correct words.

My school is modern and it's got a great [0] (*library*) / *hall* with lots of books. There's also a big [1] *canteen* / *gym* and the students have lunch there. The teachers usually eat in the [2] *computer room* / *staff room*.
My favourite subject is [3] *Science* / *History* because I'm interested [4] *in* / *about* the past and how people lived many years ago. I'm also good at Geography, but I'm worried [5] *of* / *about* my exams at the end of the year.

__ / 5

3 Circle the correct answers.

0 Dolphins are ___ animals. Dogs are also clever.
[a] intelligent b tired c bored

1 Julia likes helping people. She's a very ___ person.
a angry b sad c kind

2 Please buy a ___ of tuna.
a can b bottle c packet

3 There's a ___ of milk in the fridge.
a packet b bar c carton

4 Can I have some ___ for my coffee?
a flour b sugar c butter

5 Apples, oranges and ___ are fruit.
a eggs b cakes c strawberries

__ / 5

Grammar

4 Complete the dialogue with the Present Simple form of the verbs.

A: What [0] *do you do* (you / do) in your free time?
B: I [1] __________ (not have) a lot of free time, but I [2] __________ (often / hang out) with Jess. She's my best friend.
A: [3] __________ (you / go) to the same school?
B: No, but we [4] __________ (usually / meet) after school.
A: Where [5] __________ (Jess / live)?
B: She [6] __________ (live) about a kilometre from my house.

__ / 6

5 Complete the sentences with the correct form of *be going to* and the verbs in brackets.

0 Hurry up! I*'m not going to wait* (not / wait) for you!
1 ______ you __________ (study) English more this year?
2 I __________ (watch) the football match on TV.
3 They __________ (not / get up) early tomorrow morning.
4 ______ he __________ (walk) to school tomorrow?

__ / 4

6 Complete the sentences with the words and phrases in the box.

~~an~~	any	is there	isn't	some	there aren't

0 There's *an* interesting story in this book.
1 __________ a dictionary in your bag?
2 Are there __________ good programmes on TV?
3 There __________ a table in the kitchen.
4 There are __________ pencils on my desk.
5 __________ any vegetables in the fridge.

__ / 5

Vocabulary __ / 15 Grammar __ / 15
Your total score __ / 30

© Pearson Education Limited 2019 PHOTOCOPIABLE

_____ _____
name   class

Vocabulary

1 Look at the pictures and complete the text.

  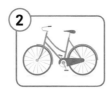
  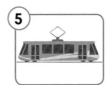

My mum is a ⁰**c**_hef_ . She works in a Greek
¹**r**_____. She hates taking the tram,
so she rides her ²**b**_____ to work.
Dad is a ³**d**_____. He works in
a ⁴**h**_____ in the centre of town.
He goes to work by ⁵**t**_____.

◯ / 5

2 Circle the correct words.

                                    ↻

My school has got a great ⁰ _hall_ /(_canteen_)
and I have lunch there every day. There's also
a modern ¹ _gym_ / _library_ with lots of books.
The teachers have a big ² _staff room_ / _playground_
and they sit there when they mark our homework.
My favourite subject is ³ _History_ / _Maths_ because
I'm interested ⁴ _of_ / _in_ numbers. I'm also good at
Science and Geography, so I'm not worried
⁵ _about_ / _in_ my exams at the end of the year.

◯ / 5

3 Circle the correct answers.

0 Dolphins are ___ animals. Dogs are also clever.
   (a) intelligent   **b** tired   **c** bored
1 There's a ___ of tuna in the cupboard.
   a bar   **b** can   **c** bottle
2 Can I have some ___ for my tea, please?
   a butter   **b** flour   **c** sugar
3 Please buy a ___ of milk.
   a carton   **b** packet   **c** jar
4 Sam is very ___. He can't find his dog.
   a funny   **b** sad   **c** kind
5 Carrrots, potatoes and ___ are vegetables.
   a biscuits   **b** cakes   **c** cucumbers

◯ / 5

Grammar

4 Complete the dialogue with the Present Simple
form of the verbs.

A: What ⁰_do you do_ (you / do) in your free time?
B: I ¹_____ (not have) a lot of free
   time, but I ²_____ (usually /
   hang out) with Martin.
A: ³_____ (Martin / live) near you?
B: Yes, he ⁴_____ (live) next door.
   We ⁵_____ (always / walk) to
   school together.
A: Where ⁶_____ (you / go) after
   school?
B: To my house or to Martin's house.

◯ / 6

5 Complete the sentences with the correct form
of _be going to_ and the verbs in brackets.

0 Hurry up! I'_m not going to wait_ (not / wait) for
   you!
1 I _____ (see) my
   grandparents next summer.
2 They _____ (not /
   watch) the tennis match on TV.
3 _____ you _____
   (study) for the test tonight?
4 _____ she _____
   (get up) early tomorrow morning?

◯ / 4

6 Complete the sentences with the words and
phrases in the box.

~~an~~   any   is there   isn't   some   there aren't

0 There's _an_ interesting story in this book.
1 There _____ a desk in my bedroom.
2 _____ a laptop in the lab?
3 _____ any eggs in the fridge.
4 There are _____ cakes on the table.
5 Are there _____ apples on the tree?

◯ / 5

Vocabulary ◯ / 15	Grammar ◯ / 15
	Your total score ◯ / 30

© Pearson Education Limited 2019   PHOTOCOPIABLE

1 Language Test A

name ______________________ class ______

Vocabulary

1 Complete the note with the words in the box.

~~animals~~ bed dishwasher living room plants table washing

Good morning, kids!
Don't forget to do the chores!
Linda, be a good girl and feed the [0]*animals*. Then water all the [1]__________.
Sam, please clear the [2]__________ after breakfast and load the [3]__________. Then vacuum the [4]__________.
Philip, please hang out the [5]__________ in the garden. And don't forget to make your [6]__________!
Mum

[ ] / [6]

2 Match 1–6 with a–f.

0 Easy-going people [g]
1 Messy people [ ]
2 Organised people [ ]
3 Patient people [ ]
4 Bossy people [ ]
5 Quiet people [ ]
6 Loud people [ ]

a don't talk a lot.
b tell everybody what to do.
c like planning everything.
d don't tidy their rooms and never know where their things are.
e can wait a long time.
f make a lot of noise.
g don't get upset easily.

[ ] / [6]

Grammar

3 Write sentences using the Present Continuous.

0 it / rain / at the moment?
Is it raining at the moment?
1 they / not / make / their beds
____
2 she / set / the table / for dinner?
____
3 I / tidy / my bedroom / right now
____
4 what / you / cooking?
____

[ ] / [4]

4 Complete the sentences with the Present Simple or the Present Continuous.

0 I *am listening* (listen) to a French song right now. I *don't understand* (not understand) the words though.
1 Tina __________ (do) a History quiz at the moment. She __________ (know) the answers to all the questions!
2 We __________ (love) sports. Right now we __________ (play) tennis.

[ ] / [4]

5 Complete the text with the Present Simple or the Present Continuous.

Mr and Mrs Thomson [0]*don't cook* (not cook) every evening, but tonight they [1]__________ (make) spaghetti and tomato sauce. Their son Jack usually [2]__________ (watch) TV before dinner, but today he [3]__________ (play) chess with his sister Lucy. Jack [4]__________ (not play) with Lucy very often. At the moment he [5]__________ (not win). He isn't happy about that!

[ ] / [5]

Communication

6 Complete the dialogues with the phrases in the box.

can I help you thank you do you need I'm sorry of course ~~can you help me~~

A: [0]*Can you help me* with the chores, please?
B: Yes, [1]__________. What can I do?

A: Can you set the table for dinner, please?
B: [2]__________, I can't. I'm busy right now.

A: [3]__________ with that heavy suitcase?
B: No, that's fine, [4]__________.

A: [5]__________ any help with the cooking?
B: Yes, please.

[ ] / [5]

Vocabulary	[ ] / [12]	Communication	[ ] / [5]
Grammar	[ ] / [13]	**Your total score**	[ ] / [30]

PHOTOCOPIABLE © Pearson Education Limited 2019

1 Language Test B

name ______________________ class ________

Vocabulary

1 Complete the note with the words in the box.

~~animals~~ bed plants rooms table
washing washing machine

Good morning, kids!
Don't forget to do the chores!
Amy, please feed the [0]animals and clear the [1]__________ after breakfast. Then vacuum the [2]__________.
Joe, be a good boy and load the [3]__________.
And don't forget to make your [4]__________!
Andy, please hang out the [5]__________ and water all the [6]__________ in the garden.
Mum

☐ / [6]

2 Match 1–6 with a–f.

0 Easy-going people [g]
1 Organised people ☐
2 Loud people ☐
3 Quiet people ☐
4 Bossy people ☐
5 Patient people ☐
6 Messy people ☐

a don't talk a lot.
b don't tidy their rooms and never know where their things are.
c like planning everything.
d tell everybody what to do.
e can wait a long time.
f make a lot of noise.
g don't get upset easily.

☐ / [6]

Grammar

3 Write sentences using the Present Continuous.

0 it / rain / at the moment?
Is it raining at the moment?
1 I / play / a game / right now
____
2 they / not set / the table
____
3 he / make / lunch / for the family?
____
4 what / you / watch?
____

☐ / [4]

4 Complete the sentences with the Present Simple or the Present Continuous.

0 I *am listening* (listen) to a French song right now. I *don't understand* (not understand) the words though.
1 We __________ (do) a Geography quiz at the moment. We __________ (know) the answers to all the questions!
2 Jack __________ (play) football right now. He __________ (love) sports.

☐ / [4]

5 Complete the text with the Present Simple or the Present Continuous.

Mr and Mrs Robinson [0] *don't cook* (not cook) every evening, but tonight they [1]__________ (make) burgers and chips. Their daughter Emma usually [2]__________ (do) her homework before dinner, but tonight she [3]__________ (not study). She [4]__________ (watch) a film on TV. She [5]__________ (not do) this very often, but her favourite actor is in the film.

☐ / [5]

Communication

6 Complete the dialogues with the phrases in the box.

can I help you that's fine do you need
I'm sorry no problem ~~can you help me~~

A: [0]*Can you help me* with the chores, please?
B: [1]__________. What can I do?

A: [2]__________ with your homework?
B: Yes, please.

A: [3]__________ any help with that sofa?
B: No, [4]__________, thank you.

A: Can you set the table for lunch, please?
B: [5]__________, I can't. I'm busy right now.

☐ / [5]

Vocabulary	☐ / [12]	Communication	☐ / [5]
Grammar	☐ / [13]	**Your total score**	☐ / [30]

© Pearson Education Limited 2019 PHOTOCOPIABLE

2 Language Test A

name ______________________ class ________

Vocabulary

1 Complete the dialogue with the words in the box.

card cash change check ~~list~~ offer queue trolley

Ben: Have you got the shopping [0] *list*, Sue?
Sue: Yes, I have. We need some apples and oranges. Let's put them in the shopping [1] ________.
Ben: Oh! Look at this chocolate. It's on special [2] ________.
Sue: Let's buy a bar. And can you [3] ________ the price of that tea?
Ben: It's quite expensive, but Mum loves it. I think we've got everything. Let's go and stand in the [4] ________.
Sue: Are you going to pay by [5] ________?
Ben: No, I prefer to pay in [6] ________.
Sue: Don't forget to get your [7] ________.

[ ] / [7]

2 Read the definitions and write the names of the shops.

This shop sells …

0 toothpaste, vitamins and shampoo. *chemist's*
1 shoes, boots and trainers. ________
2 fruit and vegetables. ________
3 magazines and newspapers. ________
4 bread and cakes. ________
5 dresses, tops and trousers. ________

[ ] / [5]

Grammar

3 Write sentences. Use the comparative form of the adjectives.

0 the supermarket / busy / the shoe shop
The supermarket is busier than the shoe shop.
1 this shop / big / that shop
____
2 books / expensive / magazines
____
3 these jeans / stylish / those trousers
____
4 my coat / warm / your jacket
____

[ ] / [4]

4 Circle the correct answer.

0 A car is [*faster*] / *the fastest* than a bicycle.
1 This dress is *longer* / *the longest* than that dress.
2 Martina is *funnier* / *the funniest* person in my class.
3 I'm *more organised* / *the most organised* than my sister.
4 Are you *better* / *the best* dancer in your family?

[ ] / [4]

5 Complete the sentences with *too*, *enough* or *as*.

0 I don't like this shop. It isn't modern *enough*.
1 I can't wear these boots. They're ________ small for me.
2 Is Marty ________ friendly as his sister?
3 The water isn't warm ________ for swimming.
4 The chocolate cake isn't as tasty ________ the apple pie.
5 You can't buy this dress. It's ________ expensive.

[ ] / [5]

Communication

6 Complete the dialogue with phrases a–f .

a Can I try it on?
~~b Can I help you?~~
c Here you are.
d I'm looking for a dress.
e The changing rooms are over there.
f Yes, we do.

Shop assistant: Good morning. [0] *b*
Customer: [1] ____ I like this one. Do you have it in blue?
Shop assistant: [2] ____ What size are you?
Customer: 10.
Shop assistant: [3] ____
Customer: Thank you. [4] ____
Shop assistant: Yes, of course. [5] ____

[ ] / [5]

Vocabulary	[ ] / [12]	Communication	[ ] / [5]
Grammar	[ ] / [13]	**Your total score**	[ ] / [30]

© Pearson Education Limited 2019 PHOTOCOPIABLE

2 Language Test B

name ______________________ class ________

Vocabulary

1 Complete the dialogue with the words in the box.

basket card cash ~~list~~ price receipt special stand

Ann: Have you got the shopping [0] *list*, Jim?
Jim: Yes, I have. We need some oranges and bananas. Can you put them in the shopping [1] ________, please? And can you check the [2] ________ of that coffee?
Ann: OK … Oh! Look at these biscuits. They're on [3] ________ offer.
Jim: Let's buy some – Dad loves them.
Ann: Well, we've got everything now. Let's go and [4] ________ in the queue.
Jim: Are you going to pay in [5] ________?
Ann: No, I prefer to pay by [6] ________.
Jim: Don't forget to get the [7] ________.

[ ] / [7]

2 Read the definitions and write the names of the shops.

This shop sells …

0 toothpaste, vitamins and shampoo. *chemist's*
1 newspapers and magazines. ________
2 tops, dresses and coats. ________
3 boots, shoes and trainers. ________
4 fruit and vegetables. ________
5 bread and cakes. ________

[ ] / [5]

Grammar

3 Write sentences. Use the comparative form of the adjectives.

0 the supermarket / busy / the shoe shop
The supermarket is busier than the shoe shop.
1 your jacket / warm / my hoodie
____
2 that shop / big / this shop
____
3 oranges / expensive / apples
____
4 those boots / stylish / these shoes
____

[ ] / [4]

4 Circle the correct answer.

0 A car is (*faster*) / *the fastest* than a bicycle.
1 James is *better* / *the best* singer in the class.
2 I'm *messier* / *the messiest* person in my family.
3 You are *more patient* / *the most patient* than your brother.
4 These trousers are *shorter* / *the shortest* than those jeans.

[ ] / [4]

5 Complete the sentences with *too*, *enough* or *as*.

0 I don't like this shop. It isn't modern *enough*.
1 You can't wear this jacket. It's ________ small for you.
2 The film isn't as funny ________ the book.
3 I can't buy these trainers. They're ________ expensive.
4 The water isn't warm ________ for swimming.
5 Is Luke ________ friendly as his brother?

[ ] / [5]

Communication

6 Complete the dialogue with phrases a–f .

a The changing rooms are over there.
~~b Can I help you?~~
c What size are you?
d Do you have it in green?
e Here you are.
f Can I try it on?

Shop assistant: Good afternoon. [0] *b*
Customer: I'm looking for a jumper. I like this one. [1] ____
Shop assistant: Yes, we do. [2] ____
Customer: Medium.
Shop assistant: [3] ____
Customer: Thank you. [4] ____
Shop assistant: Yes, of course. [5] ____

[ ] / [5]

Vocabulary	[ ] / [12]	Communication	[ ] / [5]
Grammar	[ ] / [13]	**Your total score**	[ ] / [30]

© Pearson Education Limited 2019 [PHOTOCOPIABLE]

3 Language Test A

name ______________________ class ________

Vocabulary

1 Complete the blog post with the words in the box.

camping guided explore ~~guidebook~~ hiking trips try

My family and I like doing a lot of activities when we go on holiday.

In winter, we visit different cities. We always read a [0]*guidebook* before we go. We [1]__________ the area and we go on day [2]__________ to interesting places. Sometimes we go on [3]__________ tours. In the evening, we [4]__________ the local food. It's usually yummy.

In summer, we always go [5]__________ – I love sleeping in a tent! We go [6]__________ in the mountains every day – we walk for hours.

☐ / [6]

2 Complete the sentences.

0 It's raining and I'm getting w*et*.

1 We went for a long walk and we got very t__________.

2 I need a jacket. It's getting c__________!

3 The film isn't interesting and I'm getting b__________.

4 She didn't have a map and she got l__________ in the old city.

☐ / [4]

Grammar

3 Complete the text with the Past Simple form of the verbs.

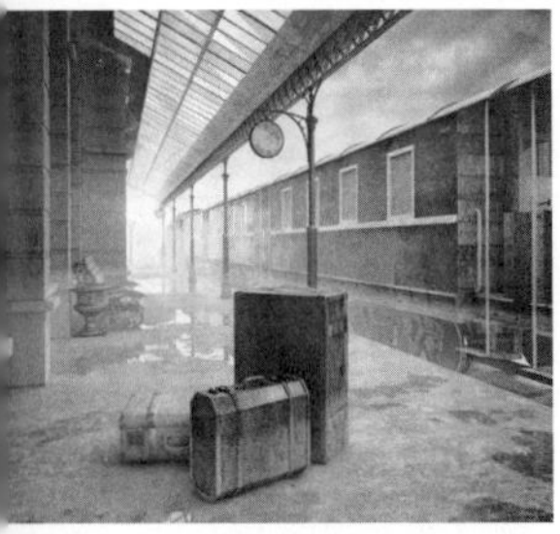

In the summer of 1923, Emily and Arthur Spencer [0] *went* (go) on holiday to the Hotel Blanc. They [1]__________ (leave) home early in the morning. They [2]__________ (meet) their friends, Julia and Basil Clifford, at the train station. The train [3]__________ (be) slow. When it [4]__________ (stop) at the first station, Basil [5]__________ (buy) a newspaper. 'Look at this!' he said. 'Something funny [6]__________ (happen) at the Hotel Blanc last night!'

☐ / [6]

4 Complete the sentences. Use the negative form of the underlined verb.

0 He went to the beach. He *didn't go* sightseeing.

1 They ate some fruit. They __________ any sandwiches.

2 I swam in the sea. I __________ in the pool.

3 The hotel was expensive. It __________ cheap.

4 She saw dolphins in the sea. She __________ whales.

☐ / [4]

5 Complete the dialogue with the Past Simple of the verbs.

Della: [0]*Did you and Fred enjoy* (you and Fred / enjoy) your holiday in Cornwall?

Jim: Yes, we [1]__________.

Della: [2]__________ (Anna / go) with you?

Jim: No, she [3]__________.

Della: How many days [4]__________ (you / be) there?

Jim: Ten days.

Della: When [5]__________ (you / arrive) back home?

Jim: Yesterday.

☐ / [5]

Communication

6 Complete the dialogues with the words and phrases in the box.

could I can't ~~can you~~ can I borrow no problem not now

A: [0] *Can you* bring me my sunglasses?
B: Yes, [1]__________.

A: [2]__________ some money from you?
B: Sorry, you [3]__________. I haven't got any money.

A: [4]__________ use the laptop, please?
B: [5]__________, sorry. I'm using it.

☐ / [5]

Vocabulary	☐ / [10]	Communication	☐ / [5]
Grammar	☐ / [15]	**Your total score**	☐ / [30]

© Pearson Education Limited 2019 PHOTOCOPIABLE

3 Language Test B

name ______________________ class ________

Vocabulary

1 Complete the blog post with the words in the box.

camping cycling explore ~~guidebook~~ guided hiking trips

My family and I like doing a lot of activities when we go on holiday. We always read a ⁰*guidebook* before we go.

In summer, we usually go ¹__________ – I love sleeping in a tent! We go ²__________ in the mountains every day – we walk for hours. We take our bikes, so we go ³__________ too.

In winter, we visit different cities. We ⁴__________ the area and we go on day ⁵__________ to interesting places. Sometimes we go on ⁶__________ tours.

[ ] / [6]

2 Complete the sentences.

0 It's raining and I'm getting w*et*.
1 It's late and it's getting d__________. I can't see.
2 The film isn't interesting and I'm getting b__________.
3 We didn't have a map and we got l__________ in the old town.
4 He went for a long walk and he got t__________.

[ ] / [4]

Grammar

3 Complete the text with the Past Simple form of the verbs.

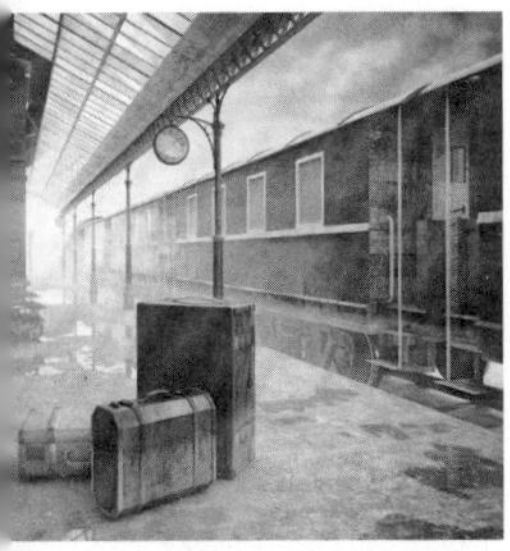

Harold and Dorothy Lewis ⁰*went* (go) on holiday to the Hotel Bellavista in the summer of 1926. They ¹__________ (meet) their friend, Charles Williams, at the train station. The train ²__________ (leave) at five minutes past seven. It ³__________ (be) very slow. At the first stop, Charles ⁴__________ (buy) a newspaper and ⁵__________ (read) the news. 'Look at this!' he said. 'Something funny ⁶__________ (happen) at the Hotel Bellavista last night!'

[ ] / [6]

4 Complete the sentences. Use the negative form of the underlined verb.

0 He went to the beach. He *didn't go* sightseeing.
1 The souvenirs were cheap. They __________ expensive.
2 They drank some water. They __________ any orange juice.
3 I saw fish in the sea. I __________ dolphins.
4 She swam in the sea. She __________ in the pool.

[ ] / [4]

5 Complete the dialogue with the Past Simple of the verbs.

Mike: ⁰*Did you and Liz enjoy* (you and Liz / enjoy) your holiday in London?
Tina: Yes, we ¹__________.
Mike: How many days ²__________ (you / be) there?
Tina: A week.
Mike: ³__________ (Liz / take) a lot of photos?
Tina: No, she ⁴__________.
Della: When ⁵__________ (you / come) back home?
Jim: Last Monday.

[ ] / [5]

Communication

6 Complete the dialogues with the words and phrases in the box.

can I borrow ~~can you~~ Could I of course you can't no

A: ⁰*Can you* bring me my sunglasses?
B: Yes, ¹__________.

A: ²__________ use your phone, please?
B: Yes, ³__________ problem.

A: ⁴__________ some money from you?
B: Sorry, ⁵__________, I haven't got any money.

[ ] / [5]

Vocabulary	[ ] / [10]	Communication	[ ] / [5]
Grammar	[ ] / [15]	**Your total score**	[ ] / [30]

© Pearson Education Limited 2019 PHOTOCOPIABLE

name _____ class _____

© Pearson Education Limited 2019 | PHOTOCOPIABLE

Vocabulary

1 Complete the sentences.

0 You use a DVD p*layer* to watch DVDs.

1 You use a **b**_____ to make smoothies with fruit and yoghurt.

2 You put a USB **s**_____ into a port on your computer or laptop.

3 You use a **r**_____ control to change the channels on your TV.

4 You use an **e**_____ toothbrush to clean your teeth.

5 You use a games **c**_____ to play computer games.

6 You use a **t**_____ to make toast.

7 You use a **m**_____ oven to warm up food or cook it.

☐ / 7

2 Complete the blog post with the words in the box.

| battery   off   ~~on~~   portable   ringtone   touch screen |

My favourite thing? My smartphone – I can't live without it! I turn my phone [0] *on* when I get up in the morning and I only turn it [1] _____ when I go to bed.

I take it everywhere! My phone's [2] _____ is old and it doesn't last long, so I take my [3] _____ charger with me too. I clean the [4] _____ every day because it gets dirty.

My phone has a great [5] _____. It's Rhianna's new song. I love it!

☐ / 5

Grammar

3 Complete the dialogue with the Past Continuous form of the verbs.

Anne: What [0] *were you doing* (you / do) last Saturday afternoon?

Mike: I [1] _____ (read) a book in the sun. My sister and brother [2] _____ (swim). [3] _____ (you and Eva / enjoy) the sunshine too?

Anne: No, we [4] _____ (not have) fun. We [5] _____ (do) chores at home.

Mike: Poor you!

☐ / 5

4 Circle the correct answer.

0 Dora *cycled /(was cycling)* to school when she saw you.

1 We *slept / were sleeping* when we heard a strange noise.

2 I was plugging in the TV when I *broke / was breaking* it.

3 Paul was jogging in the park when it *started / was starting* to rain.

4 I *dried / was drying* my hair when I dropped the hairdryer.

☐ / 4

5 Complete the sentences with adverbs of manner formed from the adjectives in brackets.

0 I don't speak French *well*, but I'm good at English. (good)

1 Our team played _____ and lost the match. (bad)

2 Please do your work _____ and don't make mistakes. (careful)

3 Joe ran very _____ because he wanted to catch the bus. (fast)

4 The man shouted _____ at the children when they broke his kitchen window. (angry)

☐ / 4

Communication

6 Complete the dialogues with the words in the box.

| happened   hear   ~~look~~   shame   what's   worried |

A: You [0] *look* upset. What [1] _____?

B: I got a bad mark in my English test.

A: I'm sorry to [2] _____ that!

....

A: You look [3] _____.

B: My dog is sick.

A: Oh, no!

....

A: [4] _____ wrong?

B: I lost my smartphone.

A: That's a [5] _____!

☐ / 5

| Vocabulary ☐ / 12 | Communication ☐ / 5 |
| Grammar ☐ / 13 | **Your total score** ☐ / 30 |

4 Language Test B

name ______________________ class ________

Vocabulary

1 Complete the sentences.

0 You use a DVD p*layer* to watch DVDs.
1 You use a **r**__________ control to change the channels on your TV.
2 You use a games **c**__________ to play computer games.
3 You use a **m**__________ oven to warm up food or cook it.
4 You use a **b**__________ to make smoothies with fruit and yoghurt.
5 You use a **t**__________ to make toast.
6 You put a USB **s**__________ into a port on your computer or laptop.
7 You use an electric **t**__________ to clean your teeth.

☐ / 7

2 Complete the blog post with the words in the box.

battery off ~~on~~ portable ringtone touch screen

I can't live without my smartphone. It's my favourite thing. I only turn it [0] *off* when I go to bed and I turn it [1] __________ in the morning. I always have it with me. I take my [2] __________ charger too because my [3] __________ is old and it doesn't last long. I clean the [4] __________ every morning because it gets dirty. My phone has got a great [5] __________, but Mum says it's too loud.

☐ / 5

Grammar

3 Complete the dialogue with the Past Continuous form of the verbs.

Judy: What [0] *were you doing* (you / do) on Friday afternoon?
Pete: It was cold, so I [1] __________ (play) computer games in my room. My brothers [2] __________ (watch) TV. [3] __________ (you and Brian / relax) too?
Judy: No, we [4] __________ (not have) fun. We [5] __________ (study) for a Maths test.
Pete: Poor you!

☐ / 5

4 Circle the correct answer.

0 Dora *cycled* / *was cycling* to school when she saw you.
1 Ron *ran* / *was running* in the park when it started to snow.
2 They were sleeping when they *heard* / *were hearing* a strange noise.
3 I *had* / *was having* a shower when the water stopped.
4 Were you unplugging the computer when you *broke* / *were breaking* the screen?

☐ / 4

5 Complete the sentences with adverbs of manner formed from the adjectives in brackets.

0 I don't speak French *well*, but I'm good at English. (good)
1 Please don't drive too __________. It's dangerous. (fast)
2 I did my homework __________ and I didn't make any mistakes. (careful)
3 The football team played __________ and lost the match. (bad)
4 The little girl laughed __________ when she saw her birthday present. (happy)

☐ / 4

Communication

6 Complete the dialogues with the words in the box.

~~look~~ shame terrible upset what wrong

A: You [0] *look* worried. What's [1] __________?
B: My cat is sick.
A: Oh no! That's [2] __________!

A: You look [3] __________.
B: I got a bad mark in my History test.
A: That's a [4] __________!

A: [5] __________ happened?
B: I can't find my dog.
A: Oh, no!

☐ / 5

Vocabulary	☐ / 12	Communication	☐ / 5
Grammar	☐ / 13	**Your total score**	☐ / 30

© Pearson Education Limited 2019 PHOTOCOPIABLE

5 Language Test A

name _____ class _____

© Pearson Education Limited 2019 | PHOTOCOPIABLE

Vocabulary

1 Complete the flu poster.

Have you got the flu?
Check:

- Have you got a high ⁰t*emperature* and a ¹h_____?
- Have you got a ²s_____ throat?
- Have you got a ³r_____ nose or a ⁴b_____ nose?
- Do ⁵s_____ and ⁶c_____ a lot?

What to do: Rest and visit your doctor!

☐ / 6

2 Look at the pictures and complete the sentences with the words in the box.

| ~~broken~~ bruise burn cut bites |

0 a *broken* leg   3 a _____
1 a _____   4 a _____
2 mosquito _____

☐ / 4

3 Circle the correct answer.

0 When you exercise, your (muscles become)/ blood becomes bigger and stronger.
1 The *heart / bone* is a big muscle and it beats about 100,000 times a day.
2 *The brain / Blood* is red and it goes to all parts of the body.
3 The *hearts / bones* in your legs and arms are the longest in your body.
4 Do intelligent animals have a big *brain / blood*?

☐ / 4

Grammar

4 Write sentences with the correct form of *have to*.

0 I / go / ✓   *I have to go* to bed early.
1 we / water / ✗
_____ the plants.
2 Dora / do / ?
_____ a lot of chores?
3 Mum / work / ✓
_____ on Saturdays.
4 they / study / ?
_____ for a test?
5 John / walk / ✗
_____ to school.
6 where / you / go / ?
_____ today?

☐ / 6

5 Complete the sentences with *should* or *shouldn't* and the verbs in brackets.

0 In tropical countries, you *should sleep* (sleep) under a mosquito net.
1 You _____ (drink) a lot of water when it's hot.
2 You _____ (go) swimming in this river. The water is very dirty.
3 '_____ (I / leave) the rubbish here?' 'No, you _____ .'
4 You _____ (put) up your tent in a safe place.

☐ / 5

Communication

6 Match 1–5 with a–e.

0 A: I feel ill and I've got a temperature. B: *f*
1 A: You should go to bed. B: ___
2 A: I've got a stomachache. B: ___
3 A: What's the matter? B: ___
4 A: I've got a burn on my hand. B: ___
5 A: I've got a headache. B: ___

a I have a terrible headache.
b Put some cream on it.
c That's a good idea.
d You should drink some mint tea.
e Why don't you lie down?
f I think you should see a doctor.

☐ / 5

| Vocabulary ☐ / 14 | Communication ☐ / 5 |
| Grammar ☐ / 11 | **Your total score** ☐ / 30 |

name _____ class _____

Vocabulary

1 Complete the flu poster.

> ### Have you got the flu?
> **Check:**
> - Have you got a high ⁰_temperature_ and a ¹h_____?
> - Do you ²c_____ and ³s_____ a lot?
> - Have you got a ⁴s_____ throat?
> - Have you have a ⁵r_____ nose or a ⁶b_____ nose?
>
> **What to do:** Rest and visit your doctor!

☐ / 6

2 Look at the pictures and complete the sentences with the words in the box.

~~broken~~ bruise burn cut bites

0 a _broken_ leg   3 a _____
1 a _____   4 mosquito _____
2 a _____

☐ / 4

3 Circle the correct answer.

0 When you exercise, your ⟨muscles become⟩/ blood becomes bigger and stronger.
1 The _hearts / bones_ in your legs and arms are the longest in your body.
2 The _bone / heart_ is a big muscle and it beats about 100,000 times a day.
3 Do intelligent animals have a big _brain / blood_?
4 _Blood / Bone_ is red and it goes to all parts of the body.

☐ / 4

Grammar

4 Write sentences with the correct form of _have to_.

0 I / go / ✓   _I have to go_ to bed early.
1 you / water / ✗
_____ the plants.
2 Phil / help / ?
_____ his mum at home?
3 Dad / make / ✓
_____ dinner tonight.
4 we / study / ?
_____ for a test?
5 Celia / take / ✗
_____ the bus to school.
6 what / you / do / ?
_____ this evening?

☐ / 6

5 Complete the sentences with _should_ or _shouldn't_ and the verbs in brackets.

0 In tropical countries, you _should sleep_ (sleep) under a mosquito net.
1 '_____ (we / put) up our tent here?' 'Yes, you _____.'
2 You _____ (swim) in this lake. The water is very dirty.
3 You _____ (drink) a lot of water when it's hot and you _____ (sit) in the sun.

☐ / 5

Communication

6 Match 1–5 with a–e.

0 A: I feel ill and I've got a temperature.   B: _f_
1 A: What's the matter?   B: ___
2 A: I've got a bad headache.   B: ___
3 A: You should go to bed.   B: ___
4 A: I've got toothache.   B: ___
5 A: I've got a cut on my finger.   B: ___

a I have earache.
b I think you should see the dentist.
c Put a plaster on it.
d That's a good idea.
e Why don't you lie down?
f You should see a doctor.

☐ / 5

Vocabulary ☐ / 14	Communication ☐ / 5
Grammar ☐ / 11	**Your total score** ☐ / 30

© Pearson Education Limited 2019

PHOTOCOPIABLE

name _____ class _____

Vocabulary

1 Circle the correct answer.

Butter biscuits

100g sugar
200g butter
300g flour

⁰*Boil /* (*Beat*) the butter and sugar together in a big ¹*oven / bowl.* ²*Add / Slice* the flour and ³*mix / fry* well. Make 15 small round biscuits. ⁴*Roast / Bake* them in the ⁵*pot / oven* (160°C) for 15–20 minutes. The biscuits are ready when they are brown.

◯/ 5

2 Complete the sentences with the words in the box.

fork   ~~glass~~   mug   pan   spoon   tin

0 Can I have a *glass* of water, please?
1 You need a cake _____ to bake a cake.
2 You can cook eggs in a frying _____.
3 I always drink hot chocolate from my favourite _____.
4 You eat soup with a _____, not with a _____.

◯/ 5

3 Complete the sentences.

0 Mum is a great cook. All her meals are d e l i c i o u s.
1 I don't like lemons or other s _ _ _ fruit.
2 There's a lot of sugar in these biscuits. They're too s _ _ _ _ _.
3 The restaurant has a dirty kitchen and the food is d _ _ _ _ _ _ _ _ _ _ _. Don't eat it.
4 The pasta has tomato sauce with chillies. It's very s _ _ _ _ _!

◯/ 4

Grammar

4 Complete the note with the Present Perfect form of the verbs.

Hi Mum!
Andy and I ⁰*have had* (have) breakfast.
We ¹_____ (not cleaned) the kitchen, but I ²_____ (put) the food back in the fridge.
Andy ³_____ (not load) the dishwasher, but he ⁴_____ (make) his bed. Gran ⁵_____ (leave) a note for you.
See you this evening!
Love you!
Sarah

◯/ 5

5 Write the Present Perfect questions and answers.

0 he / wash / the dirty floor? (✓)
  A: *Has he washed the dirty floor?*
  B: *Yes, he has.*
1 they / ever / be / on TV? (✓)
  A: _____
  B: _____
2 she / buy / the vegetables? (✓)
  A: _____
  B: _____
3 you / ever / eat / Mexican food? (✗)
  A: _____
  B: _____

◯/ 6

Communication

6 Circle the correct answer.

A: Would you ⁰(*like to*)/ *like* go to the cinema or watch a DVD?
B: You ¹*prefer / choose.*

A: Pizza with mushrooms or pizza with ham?
B: I ²*like / don't mind.*

A: ³*I'd like to / I'd like* go home now.
B: Me too.

A: Would you ⁴*like / mind* a salad or fruit?
B: ⁵*I'm / I'd prefer* fruit.

◯/ 5

| Vocabulary ◯/ 14 | Communication ◯/ 5 |
| Grammar ◯/ 11 | **Your total score** ◯/ 30 |

© Pearson Education Limited 2019   PHOTOCOPIABLE

name _____ class _____

Vocabulary

1 Circle the correct answer.

Butter biscuits

100g sugar
200g butter
300g flour

⁰*Boil* / *Beat* the butter and sugar together in a big ¹*oven* / *bowl*. ²*Slice* / *Add* the flour and ³*roast* / *mix* well. Make 12 small round biscuits. ⁴*Bake* / *Fry* them in the ⁵*pot* / *oven* (160°C) for 15–20 minutes. The biscuits are ready when they are brown.

◯ / 5

2 Complete the sentences with the words in the box.

~~cup~~   glass   knife   pot   spoon   tin

0 He always drinks coffee in this *cup*.
1 Make some chicken soup in a big _____ .
2 You need a sharp _____ to cut meat.
3 You eat ice cream with a _____ .
4 You need a cake _____ to bake a cake.
5 I always have a _____ of orange juice for breakfast.

◯ / 5

3 Complete the sentences.

0 Mum is a great cook. All her meals are d e l i c i o u s .
1 Put some salt on this popcorn. It isn't s _ _ _ _ _ enough.
2 The pizza has chillies on it. It's too s _ _ _ _ _ for me.
3 The fish smells really bad. It's d _ _ _ _ _ _ _ _ _ .
4 Green apples, and lemons are s _ _ _ .

◯ / 4

Grammar

4 Complete the note with the Present Perfect form of the verbs.

Hi Mum!
Cindy and I ⁰*have had* (have) our breakfast. Cindy
¹_____ (make) a pie for you and Dad.
She ²_____ (not put) in the fridge, she
³_____ (leave) it in the oven.
We ⁴_____ (not clean) the kitchen but
I ⁵_____ (load) the dishwasher.
See you later!
Love you!
Jack

◯ / 5

5 Write the Present Perfect questions and answers.

0 he / wash / the dirty floor? (✓)
  A: *Has he washed the dirty floor?*
  B: *Yes, he has.*
1 you / ever / be / on TV? (✗)
  A: _____
  B: _____
2 they / ever / eat / pasta with pesto? (✗)
  A: _____
  B: _____
3 she / buy / the fruit? (✓)
  A: _____
  B: _____

◯ / 6

Communication

6 Circle the correct answer.

A: Would you ⁰*like to* / *like* go to the cinema or watch a DVD?
B: I ¹*don't mind* / *choose*.

A: Would you ²*like* / *like to* fish or meat?
B: ³*I'm* / *I'd* prefer fish, please.

A: Eggs with ham or tomatoes?
B: You ⁴*choose* / *like*.

A: ⁵*I prefer* / *I'd like* to have lunch now.
B: Me too.

◯ / 5

| Vocabulary ◯ / 14 | Communication ◯ / 5 |
| Grammar ◯ / 11 | **Your total score** ◯ / 30 |

© Pearson Education Limited 2019   PHOTOCOPIABLE

name ______________________ class ________

Vocabulary

1 Complete the texts with the words in the box.

attic balcony block cottage floor ~~island~~ stairs village

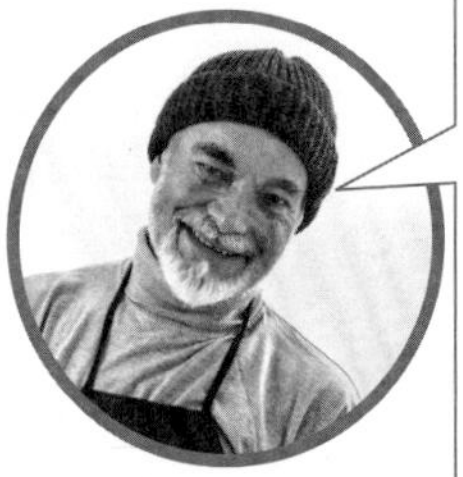

I love living on an [0]*island*. My home is a pretty [1]__________ near the beach. I can see the sea from a window up in the [2]__________. I don't have any neighbours, but my best friend lives in a small [3]__________ about a kilometre away.

Our [4]__________ of flats is in a town. We live on the fourth [5]__________ and we usually walk up the [6]__________. It's good exercise. We have a [7]__________ and we sit on it when the weather is good.

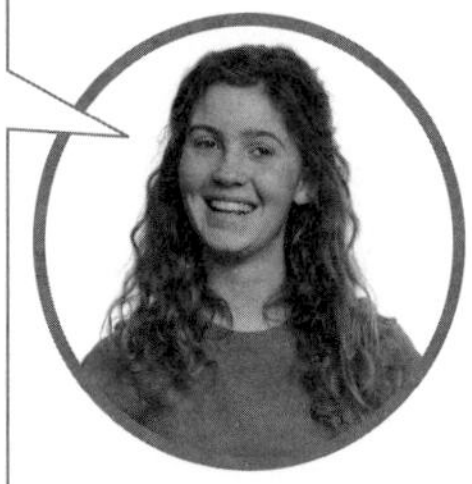

☐ / 7

2 Complete the sentences.

0 I found the book I wanted in the b*ookcase*.
1 I put the dirty glasses in the kitchen s _ _ _.
2 Look at your face in the m _ _ _ _ _! It's dirty.
3 I turned on the hot water t _ _ because I wanted to have a bath.
4 I keep the flour, sugar, salt and pasta in that c _ _ b _ _ _ _.

☐ / 4

3 Circle the correct answer.

0 What time is Dad picking *out* / *up* the children from school?
1 Check *for* / *out* this article. It's very interesting.
2 I made a cake and then cleaned *up* / *in* the mess.
3 She was looking *for* / *out* her cat but she didn't find him.
4 You should find *out* / *for* about the history of your town.

☐ / 4

Grammar

4 Complete the dialogues with the correct Present Continuous form of the verbs.

A: [0]*Are you walking* (you / walk) home after school?
B: No, I'm not. I [1]__________ (go) to town with Mandy.

A: [2]__________ (Joe / study) this afternoon?
B: No, he isn't. He [3]__________ (play) chess with Sue.

A: [4]__________ (Amy and Fred / come) to the party?
B: No, they aren't. They [5]__________ (move) house on Saturday.

☐ / 5

5 Circle the correct answer.

0 The children *can* / *must* watch TV, but not after ten o'clock.
1 You *must* / *mustn't* play football in the street. It's very dangerous.
2 I *can* / *must* phone my parents. It's important.
3 The students *must* / *mustn't* study now. They have an exam tomorrow.
4 We *must* / *mustn't* leave our rubbish on the beach.
5 *Can* / *Must* I borrow your hairdryer? I haven't got one.

☐ / 5

Communication

6 Complete the dialogues with the phrases.

are you free can you come I can't ~~do you want to~~ I'd love to that sounds

A: [0]*Do you want to* hang out on Sunday?
B: [1]__________ great.

A: [2]__________ on Friday evening? Would you like to hang out?
B: Yes, [3]__________, thanks.

A: We're going to the zoo tomorrow. [4]__________?
B: Sorry, [5]__________.

☐ / 5

Vocabulary	☐ / 15	Communication	☐ / 5
Grammar	☐ / 10	**Your total score**	☐ / 30

© Pearson Education Limited 2019 PHOTOCOPIABLE

7 Language Test B

name ______________________ class ________

Vocabulary

1 Complete the texts with the words in the box.

attic basement city cottage detached ground ~~island~~ village

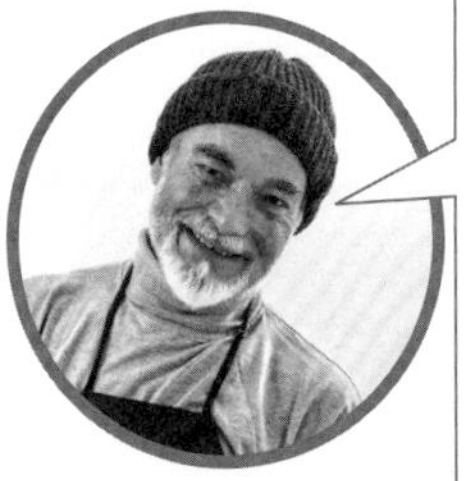

I love living on an [0]*island*. My home is a beautiful little [1]__________. I don't have any neighbours, but my best friend lives in a [2]__________ about a kilometre away. The sea is near too. I can see the sea from a window in my [3]__________.

We live in a [4]__________ house in a big [5]__________. There's a kitchen, a dining room and a living room on the [6]__________ floor and four bedrooms and two bathrooms on the first floor. There's also a [7]__________ under the house.

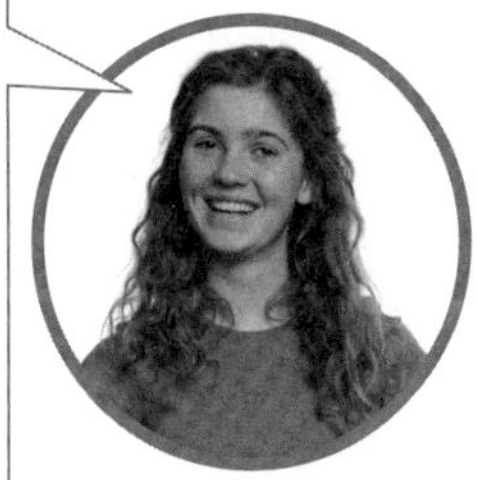

☐ / 7

2 Complete the sentences.

0 I found the book I wanted in the **b** *o o k c a s e*.
1 My mum keeps the cups, mugs and glasses in this **c** _ **p** _ _ _ _ _.
2 I put the dirty glasses in the kitchen **s** _ _ _.
3 His desk has a big **d** _ _ _ _ _ _. There are pencils in there.
4 She looked at her hair in the **m** _ _ _ _ _. It was beautiful.

☐ / 4

3 Circle the correct answer.

0 What time is Dad picking *out* / (*up*) the children from school?
1 What happened? Did you find *out* / *for*?
2 I go to bed very late, so I wake *in* / *up* late too.
3 Please clean *in* / *up* the mess on the floor before Mum sees it.
4 I'm looking *for* / *in* my glasses. Can you see them?

☐ / 4

Grammar

4 Complete the dialogues with the correct Present Continuous form of the verbs.

A: [0]*Are you going* (you / go) home after school?
B: No, I'm not. I [1]__________ (take) the bus to town with Luke.

A: [2]__________ (Tony / do) his homework this afternoon?
B: No, he isn't. He [3]__________ (meet) Anne at the gym.

A: [4]__________ (Ben and Sally / study) this evening?
B: No, they aren't. They [5]__________ (visit) their grandparents.

☐ / 5

5 Circle the correct answer.

0 The children (*can*) / *must* watch TV, but not after ten o'clock.
1 You *mustn't* / *can* tell your friends. It's a secret.
2 *Must* / *Can* I use your phone? I need to call Mum.
3 We *must* / *mustn't* make a noise. Dad is sleeping.
4 The students *must* / *can* do their homework or the teacher gets angry.
5 You *mustn't* / *can* use my laptop, no problem.

☐ / 5

Communication

6 Complete the dialogues with the phrases.

would you like are you free ~~do you want to~~ I'd love to maybe next time that sounds

A: [0]*Do you want to* hang out on Sunday?
B: [1]__________ great.

A: We're going swimming tomorrow. [2]__________ to come with us?
B: Sorry, [3]__________.

A: [4]__________ this weekend? Would you like to go camping?
B: Yes, [5]__________, thanks.

☐ / 5

Vocabulary	☐ / 15	Communication	☐ / 5
Grammar	☐ / 10	**Your total score**	☐ / 30

© Pearson Education Limited 2019 PHOTOCOPIABLE

8 Language Test A

name ________________ class ________

Vocabulary

1 Circle the correct answer.

When I was at school, I wanted to [0] (*be*) / *am* a writer. I wanted to [1] *go* / *have* an interesting job. I decided to learn [2] *foreign* / *famous* languages because they are very useful when you travel. When I was older, I went to live [3] *abroad* / *here* and wrote books. I didn't want to live on my [4] *own* / *one*. I wanted to [5] *have* / *be* a family. One day ...

☐ / [5]

2 Complete the text with the words in the box.

hands hug ~~invited~~ kissed visiting

I made a new friend last week. His name is Charlie. He [0] *invited* me to his house and I met his family. They were very friendly. I shook [1] __________ with his dad and his mum [2] __________ me. When I left, she gave me a [3] __________ and asked me to come again. Next weekend, Charlie is [4] __________ me and it will be his turn to meet my family.

☐ / [4]

3 Complete the text.

Nigel is a very annoying boy. He never [0] a *r r i v e* s anywhere on time. He's always [1] l _ _ _. He borrows things and he never [2] a _ _ s for permission. He [3] i _ _ _ _ _ _ _ _ _ s people all the time when they are talking. He never [4] w _ _ _ s his turn to use the bathroom. Someone should tell him to be more [5] p _ _ _ _ _!

☐ / [4]

Grammar

4 Complete the sentences. Use the correct form of *will* and the verbs in brackets

0 I *will have* (have) my own business one day.
1 Dad ______________ (not get) to work on time.
2 ______________ (you / go) to university when you're older?
3 Max ______________ (not be) a famous actor.
4 ______________ (they / win) the match?
5 I hope I ______________ (be) happy in the future.
6 Where ______________ (you / live) in the future?

☐ / [6]

5 Complete the dialogue using the correct question words and verbs.

Olivia: Hi Zoe. [0] *How are* you?
Zoe: Fine, but I'm busy. I'm doing some work.
Olivia: But we're on holiday! [1] __________ __________ you working?
Zoe: Because I want to post a new blog entry.
Olivia: [2] __________ __________ __________ you write your blog?
Zoe: Every day if I can.
Olivia: I came back from London yesterday.
Zoe: [3] __________ __________ you doing there?
Olivia: I was visiting my friend Erica. She took me to some cool places.
Zoe: [4] __________ __________ she take you?
Olivia: To the zoo, Madame Tussaud's, some great clothes shops…
Zoe: Wow! That sounds great! [5] __________ __________ you visiting us again?
Olivia: I'm not sure. We've got visitors next week.
Zoe: Really? [6] __________ __________ coming?
Olivia: My cousin. Why don't you come to *my* house? Then we can all hang out together.
Zoe: Great. See you soon.

☐ / [6]

Communication

6 Complete the dialogues with the phrases in the box.

~~I agree~~ I disagree I don't think that isn't that's true that's what

0 A: Vicky is a great singer.
B: *I agree* with you. I love all her songs.
1 A: Tokyo is smaller than London.
B: ______________ right. Tokyo is bigger.
2 A: Our computer is old and it's too slow.
B: ______________. We have to buy a new one.
3 A: Maths is a very difficult subject.
B: ______________ so. I think it's easy.
4 A: Shopping for clothes is boring.
B: ______________ I think too. I hate it.
5 A: The film was better than the book.
B: ______________ with you. The book was great!

☐ / [5]

Vocabulary	☐ / [13]	Communication	☐ / [5]
Grammar	☐ / [12]	**Your total score**	☐ / [30]

© Pearson Education Limited 2019 PHOTOCOPIABLE

name _____ class _____

Vocabulary

1 Circle the correct answer.

When I was at school, I wanted to ⁰go /(have)
an interesting job. I wanted to ¹be / am a writer
and travel around the world, so I decided to
learn ²famous / foreign languages. When I was
older, I lived ³here / abroad and I wrote articles
for magazines. I didn't want to live on my ⁴now /
own. I wanted to ⁵have / be a family. One day …

☐ / 5

2 Complete the text with the words in the box.

| hands hug ~~invited~~ kissed visiting |

Mandy is my new friend. She's great! Last week, she
⁰ invited me to her house and I met her family.
They were very friendly. Her mum ¹_____ me
and gave me a ²_____ . I shook ³_____
with her dad. When I left, her parents asked me
to come again. Mandy is ⁴_____ me next
weekend and it will be her turn to meet my family.

☐ / 4

3 Complete the text.

Arthur is a very annoying boy. He never
⁰a r r i v e s anywhere on time. He's always
¹l _ _ _ _. When people are talking, he
²i _ _ _ _ _ _ _ _ s them all the time. He never
³a _ _ s for permission when he borrows things.
He never waits his ⁴t _ _ _ _ to use the bathroom.
I think he should be more ⁵p _ _ _ _ _ _!

☐ / 4

Grammar

**4 Complete the sentences. Use the correct form
of will and the verbs in brackets**

0 I will have (have) my own business one day.

1 Lisa _____ (not be) a famous actor.

2 Where _____ (you / live) in the future?

3 _____ (you / buy) a house on an
island one day?

4 Mum _____ (not arrive) at work on
time.

5 _____ (they / pass) all their exams?

6 I hope I _____(be) happy in the
future.

☐ / 6

**5 Complete the dialogue using the correct
question words and verbs.**

Matt: Hi Jack. ⁰How are you?

Jack: Fine, thanks. I came back from London
yesterday.

Matt: ¹_____ _____ you doing there?

Jack: My sister and I were visiting my uncle. He
took us to some cool places.

Matt: ²_____ _____ you go?

Jack: We went to Madame Tussaud's and the zoo.

Matt: Wow! What a great trip.

Jack: Do you want to hang out this afternoon?

Matt: Sorry, I can't. I'm busy.

Jack: ³_____ _____ you busy?

Matt: Because we're fixing my dad's motorbike.

Jack: I didn't know he's got a motorbike.
⁴_____ _____ _____ he ride
it?

Matt: He rides it every weekend.

Jack: ⁵_____ _____ you having the
barbecue?

Matt: This Saturday. I also invited some other
people to the barbecue.

Jack: ⁶_____ _____ you invite?

Matt: I invited our new neighbours.

Jack: Great. See you on Saturday.

☐ / 6

Communication

**6 Complete the dialogues with the phrases in the
box.**

| ~~I agree~~ I disagree I don't think
that isn't that's true that's what |

0 A: Vicky is a great singer.
   B: I agree with you. I love all her songs.

1 A: The concert wasn't very good.
   B: _____ with you. The singer was great!

2 A: History is a boring subject.
   B: _____ so. I think it's interesting.

3 A: Canada is the biggest country in the world.
   B: _____ right. Russia is bigger.

4 A: I can't fix this car. It's too old.
   B: _____ . Maybe we can buy a new one.

5 A: Dogs are the best pets.
   B: _____ I think too. I love them.

☐ / 5

| Vocabulary ☐ / 13 | Communication ☐ / 5 |
| Grammar ☐ / 12 | **Your total score** ☐ / 30 |

© Pearson Education Limited 2019 PHOTOCOPIABLE

name _____ class _____

Listening

1 🔊 **2** Listen and complete the sentences with one word or a number.

0 Mum wants to buy Grandad a *stylish* jacket.
1 The jacket in the department store costs £_____.
2 The shirt is dark _____.
3 Grandad's size is _____.
4 Mum can pay for the jacket by _____.
5 The café is next to the _____.

☐ / ⑤

2 🔊 **3** Listen and circle the correct answer.

0 a Colin is younger than Eddie.
　 b Colin is as old as Eddie.
1 a Eddie is bossy.
　 b Colin is bossy.
2 a Eddie is a quieter person than Colin.
　 b Colin is a quieter person than Eddie.
3 a Eddie is as intelligent as Colin.
　 b Eddie is more intelligent than Colin.
4 a Colin a messy person.
　 b Eddie is a messy person.
5 a Eddie is better than Colin at football.
　 b Colin is better than Eddie at football.

☐ / ⑤

Communication

3 **Look at the pictures. Match sentences a–g to situations 1–5. There two extra sentences.**

0 ⓗ  **1** ☐

2 ☐  **3** ☐

4 ☐  **5** ☐

a Can I help you with your homework?
b I'm sorry, I can't. I'm busy right now.
c Here you are, size 10.
d Do you need any help with the armchair?
e Put away these shirts, please.
f The changing rooms are over there.
g Do you have these in a small?
h No, thanks. I'm just looking.

☐ / ⑤

© Pearson Education Limited 2019 | PHOTOCOPIABLE

name _____   class _____

Reading

4 Read Marty's blog and write T (true) or F (false).

HOME | ABOUT ME | CONTACT

Saturday chores!
by Marty Winston

My Saturday mornings begin at half past six. I like getting up early. I have a shower, make my bed and tidy my room. I do this every day. Then I set the table and make breakfast. I make pancakes for my brother Jamie and my sister Anna, eggs for Dad, toast for Mum, tea and orange juice. I'm the best cook in my family! (I want to be a chef one day.)

After breakfast, I load the washing machine: white clothes first and then clothes with dark colours. Mum doesn't want my brother to do this chore. A week ago, he washed his red shirt with some white clothes. Now we've got pink socks and pink T-shirts!

My brother Jamie and my sister Anna get up at nine. They hate getting up early. They have chores too. Anna takes the clothes out of the washing machine and hangs them out. Then she vacuums the rooms. Jamie feeds our dogs, brushes them and takes them for a walk. The animals love Jamie and he's very patient with them. He also takes out the rubbish at night. He hates this job!

---

0 Marty gets up early in the morning on Saturdays. `T`

1 Marty makes his bed and tidies his room once a week. ☐

2 Marty's mum has pancakes for breakfast. ☐

3 After breakfast, Marty does one more chore. ☐

4 Marty's brother gets up later than Marty. ☐

5 Jamie doesn't look after the family's pets. ☐

☐ / 5

5 Complete the text with the words in the box.

at   baker's   enough   is   than   ~~usually~~

My family and I are **0**_usually_ at home on Saturday mornings, but not this weekend. **1**_____ the moment, Mum is in town with Dad. He wants a new laptop because his old one isn't fast **2**_____! My sister is at the **3**_____. She **4**_____ buying some bread and apple pies. They're nicer **5**_____ the ones at the supermarket. I'm in the park with my friends because I hate shopping!

☐ / 5

Writing

6 Write 70–80 words about your Saturdays. Use these questions to help you.

1 What time do you usually get up on Saturdays?
2 What household chores do you do?
3 What chores do the other members of your family do?
4 Do you go shopping on Saturdays?
5 What other things do you do on Saturdays?

_____
_____
_____
_____
_____
_____
_____
_____
_____
_____
_____
_____
_____
_____

☐ / 5

© Pearson Education Limited 2019   PHOTOCOPIABLE

Listening ☐ / 10	Communication ☐ / 5
Reading ☐ / 10	Writing ☐ / 5
	Your total score ☐ / 30

1&2 Skills Test B

name ______________________ class ______

Listening

1 🔊 2 Listen and complete the sentences with one word or a number.

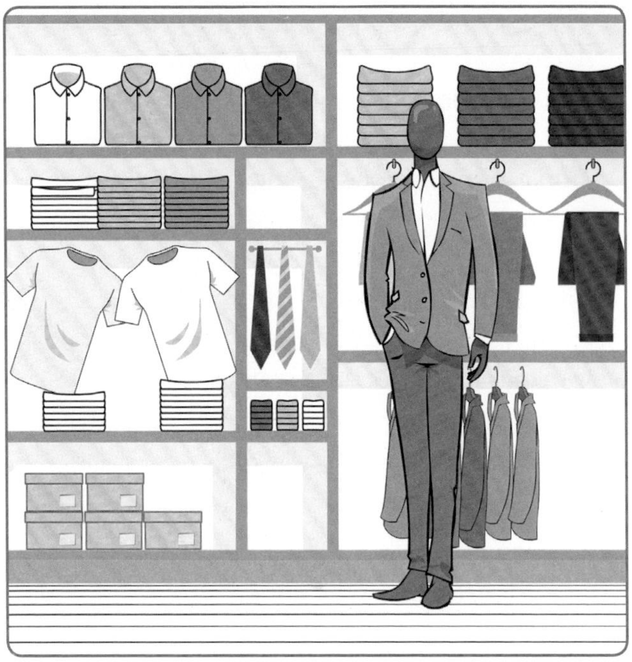

0 Mum wats to buy Grandad a *stylish* jacket.
1 The jacket in the department store is too ________.
2 The clothes shop is next to the ________.
3 The shirt costs £________.
4 Stella can pay for the shirt in ________.
5 Mum and Stella are going to have lunch at the ________.

☐ / 5

2 🔊 3 Listen and circle the correct answer.

0 a Colin is younger than Eddie.
  [b] Colin is as old as Eddie.
1 a Eddie often gets angry.
  b Eddie never gets angry.
2 a Colin is a quieter person than Eddie.
  b Eddie is a quieter person than Colin.
3 a Colin is more intelligent than Eddie.
  b Colin is as intelligent as Eddie.
4 a Eddie is a tidy person.
  b Colin is a tidy person.
5 a Colin is better than Eddie at football.
  b Eddie is better than Colin at football.

☐ / 5

Communication

3 Look at the pictures. Match sentences a–g to situations 1–5. There two extra sentences.

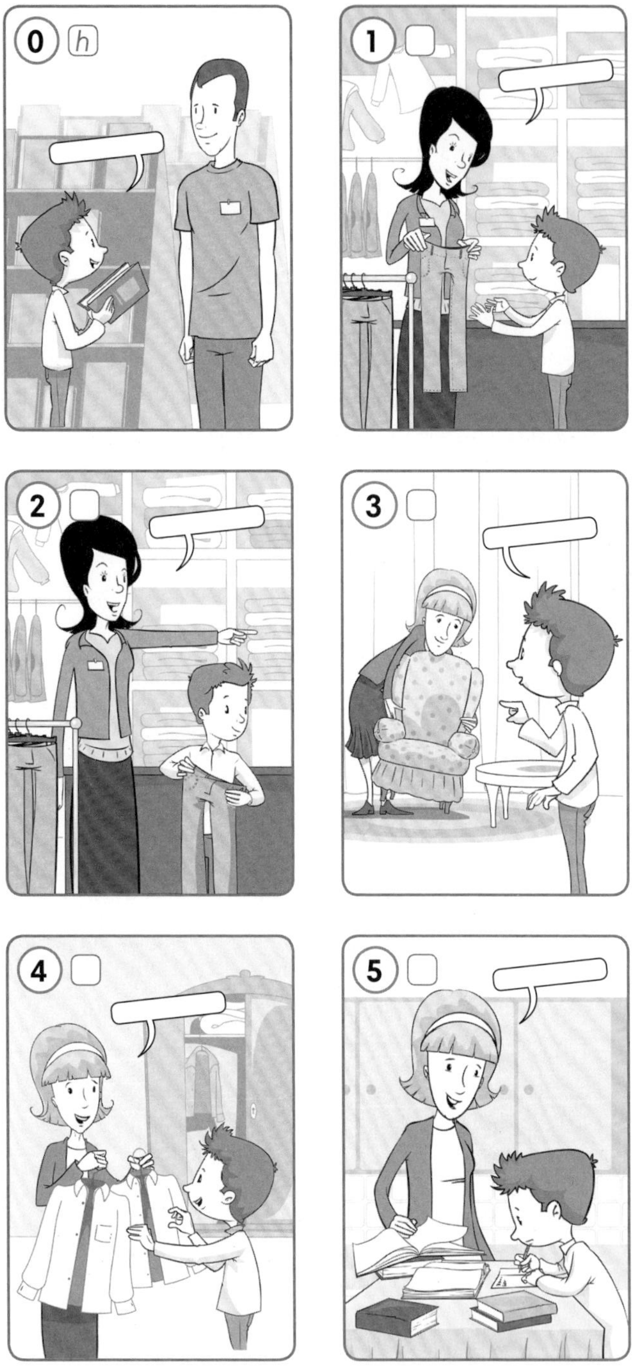

a Do you need any help with the armchair?
b Put away these shirts, please.
c Do you have these in black?
d Can I help you with your homework?
e I'm sorry, I can't. I'm busy right now.
f Here you are, size 8.
g The changing rooms are over there.
h No, thanks. I'm just looking.

☐ / 5

© Pearson Education Limited 2019 PHOTOCOPIABLE

Skills Test B

name _______________ class _______

Reading

4 Read Helen's blog and write T (true) or F (false).

HOME | ABOUT ME | CONTACT

Saturday chores!

by Helen Marsden

My Saturday mornings begin at half past six. I like it getting up early. I have a shower, make my bed and tidy my room. I do this every day. Then I set the table and make breakfast. I make pancakes for my sister Jessica and my brother Andy, eggs for Mum, toast for Dad, coffee and orange juice. I'm the best cook in my family! (I want to be a chef one day.)

After breakfast, I load the washing machine: white clothes first and then clothes with dark colours. Mum doesn't want my brother to do this chore. A week ago, he washed his red shirt with some white clothes. Now we've got pink socks and pink T-shirts!

My brother and my sister get up at nine. They hate getting up early. They have chores too. Jessica takes the clothes out of the washing machine and hangs them out. Then she vacuums the rooms. Andy feeds our dogs, brushes them and takes them for a walk. The animals love Andy and he's very patient with them. He also takes out the rubbish at night. He hates this job!

0 Helen gets up early in the morning on Saturdays. [*T*]
1 Helen makes her bed and tidies her room every day. [ ]
2 Helen's Dad has eggs for breakfast. [ ]
3 Helen doesn't do any more chores after breakfast. [ ]
4 Jessica and Andy get up earlier than Helen. [ ]
5 Andy looks after the family's pets. [ ]

[ ] / [5]

5 Complete the text with the words in the box.

as don't greengrocer's right too ~~usually~~

My family and I are [0] *usually* at home on Saturday mornings, but not this weekend. [1] __________ now Dad is in town with Granny. She needs a new computer because her old one is [2] __________ slow. I [3] __________ like shopping, so I'm in the park with my friends. Mum wants to buy some fruit and vegetables, so she's at the [4] __________. The food there isn't as cheap [5] __________ the food in the supermarket, but it's better.

[ ] / [5]

Writing

6 Write 70–80 words about your Saturdays. Use these questions to help you.

1 What time do you usually get up on Saturdays?
2 What household chores do you do?
3 What chores do the other members of your family do?
4 Do you go shopping for food on Saturdays?
5 What other things do you do on Saturdays?

____
____
____
____
____
____
____
____
____
____
____
____
____
____
____

[ ] / [5]

Listening	[ ] / [10]	Communication	[ ] / [5]
Reading	[ ] / [10]	Writing	[ ] / [5]
		Your total score	[ ] / [30]

© Pearson Education Limited 2019 [PHOTOCOPIABLE]

name ______________________ class ________

Listening

1 ☊ **4 Cathy is talking to her friend. Listen and write the answers to questions 1–5.**

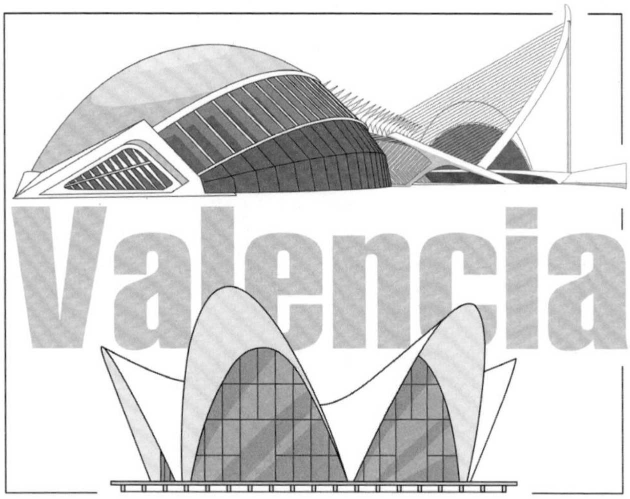

0 Where did Cathy and her family go?
To Spain

1 Who is Spanish?
____

2 Did they like the local food?
____

3 What did they do on the second day of their holiday?
____

4 Where was Anna Smart when Cathy saw her?
____

5 Where was Jack when Cathy took the selfie?
____

☐ / 5

2 ☊ **5 Listen to people talking about useful things. Match the speakers with the things a–e.**

Speaker 0	[f]	**a** DVD player
Speaker 1	☐	**b** electric toothbrush
Speaker 2	☐	**c** hairdryer
Speaker 3	☐	**d** blender
Speaker 4	☐	**e** guidebook
Speaker 5	☐	**f** USB stick

☐ / 5

Communication

3 Complete the dialogue with answers a–h. There are two extra answers.

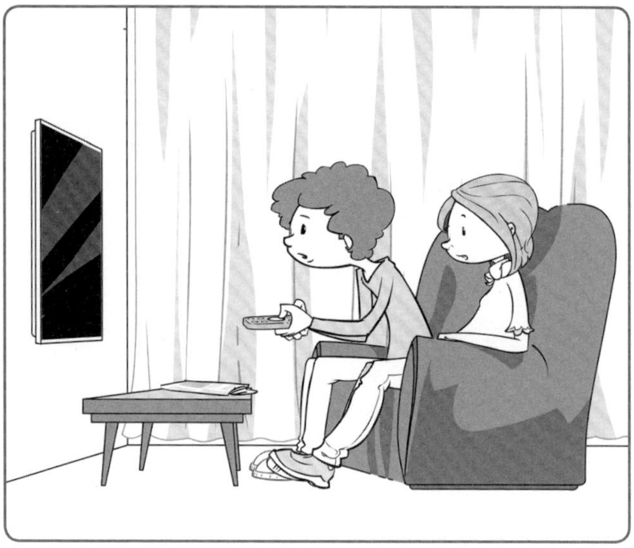

Cassie: What's wrong, Robbie?
Robbie: [0] _b_
Cassie: That's a shame … Did you plug it in?
Robbie: [1] ________
Cassie: Let's look on the Internet for help. Where's your laptop?
Robbie: [2] ________
Cassie: OK… What happens when you press the 'On' button on the remote control?
Robbie: [3] ________
Cassie: Has the remote control got batteries in?
Robbie: [4] ________
Cassie: Let me see … Oh, Robbie! There's the problem! No batteries! The TV is fine. Can you go to the shops and buy some batteries?
Robbie: [5] ________

a I didn't check, but I think it has.
b Our new smart TV isn't working.
c You look upset.
d Not now, but I can go tomorrow.
e Nothing. The TV screen is black.
f Dad is using it at the moment.
g Can I help you?
h Yes, I did. And I read the instructions carefully.

☐ / 5

© Pearson Education Limited 2019 PHOTOCOPIABLE

3&4 Skills Test A

name ______________________ class ________

Reading

4 Read Amanda's story and complete the sentences with one, two or three words.

HOME | ABOUT ME | CONTACT

MY GREEK HOLIDAY

by *Amanda Clarke*

Last month we went on holiday to Greece. We took a taxi to the airport early in the morning. Six hours later, we arrived in Athens. The sun was shining and it was very hot.

Mum was tired, so she stayed at the hotel. Dad and I were hungry, so we found a restaurant and tried the local food. I don't usually like fish, but the fish at this restaurant was delicious! Dad had a salad with cheese and tomatoes and lots of bread.

The next day we went on a guided tour of Athens. Then we met some Greek friends and explored the city together. In the evening we had dinner, listened to music and danced.

On the third day, we went on a boat trip to a small island near Athens. I was looking at the sea when I saw dolphins! They were swimming near the boat and jumping out of the water. I loved the island. There aren't any cars there, so people walk everywhere or ride donkeys!

We stayed in Greece for one week and it was fantastic.

0 Amanda and her family went to the airport by *taxi*.
1 In Athens it was ______________ and the sun was shining.
2 Mrs Clarke stayed at the hotel because ______________.
3 Amanda liked the ______________ at the restaurant.
4 The Clarke family ______________ with some Greek friends.
5 People ride donkeys or they ______________ everywhere on the island.

☐ / 5

5 Complete the email with the words in the box.

battery broke ~~go~~ oven portable was

Hi Max,
We had a terrible time last weekend! We went on a trip, but the weather was bad and we didn't [0] *go* hiking. There [1] __________ a storm and the house didn't have electricity. We didn't use the microwave [2] __________ to cook our food and there was no TV. My laptop wasn't working because the [3] __________ was dead and my [4] __________ charger was at home. I didn't text you because I dropped my mobile phone and [5] __________ the screen.
See you soon, I hope!
Ben

☐ / 5

Writing

6 Write 70–80 words about a weekend you didn't enjoy because something happened. Use these questions to help you.

1 Where were you?
2 Who was with you?
3 What were you doing when something happened?
4 What happened next?
5 What was the result and how did you feel?

____
____
____
____
____
____
____
____
____
____
____
____

☐ / 5

Listening	☐ / 10	Communication	☐ / 5
Reading	☐ / 10	Writing	☐ / 5
		Your total score	☐ / 30

© Pearson Education Limited 2019 PHOTOCOPIABLE

3&4 Skills Test B

name ______________________ class ______

Listening

1 🔊 **4 Cathy is talking to her friend. Listen and write the answers to questions 1–5.**

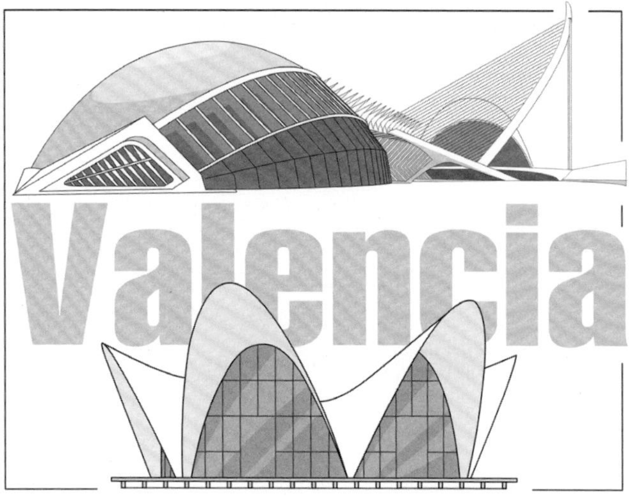

0 Where did Cathy and her family go?
To Spain

1 Did they have a good time?
____

2 Where did they stay?
____

3 What did they do on the first day of their holiday?
____

4 Where was Cathy when she saw Anna Smart?
____

5 Who was Jack with?
____

☐ / 5

2 🔊 **5 Listen to people talking about useful things. Match the speakers with the things a–e.**

Speaker 0	[f]	a	blender
Speaker 1	☐	b	guidebook
Speaker 2	☐	c	electric toothbrush
Speaker 3	☐	d	DVD player
Speaker 4	☐	e	hairdryer
Speaker 5	☐	f	USB stick

☐ / 5

Communication

3 Complete the dialogue with answers a–h. There are two extra answers.

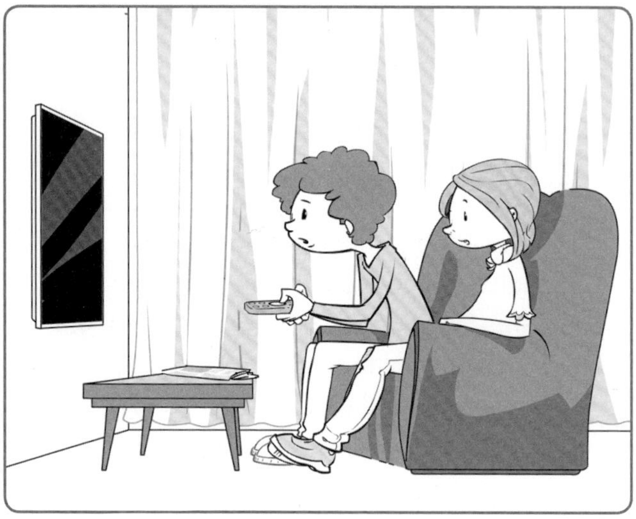

Lucy: Hi, Dave. What's wrong?
Dave: 0 *e*
Lucy: That's a shame … Did you read the instructions?
Dave: 1 ________
Lucy: Can we go online? We can read about this problem on the Internet.
Dave: 2 ________
Lucy: OK… What happens when you press the 'On' button on the remote control?
Dave: 3 ________
Lucy: Are there any batteries in the remote control?
Dave: 4 ________
Lucy: Let me see. … No batteries! The TV is fine, Dave. Can you go to the shops and buy some batteries?
Dave: 5 ________

a I didn't check, but I think there are.
b Yes, I did. And I did everything they said.
c Not now, sorry. Mum is using the laptop at the moment.
d You look worried.
e Our new smart TV isn't working.
f Can I help you?
g Nothing. The TV screen is black!
h I can't go now, but I can go tomorrow.

☐ / 5

PHOTOCOPIABLE © Pearson Education Limited 2019

name _____ class _____

Reading

4 Read Amanda's story and complete the sentences with one, two or three words.

HOME | ABOUT ME | CONTACT

MY GREEK HOLIDAY
by Amanda Clarke

Last month we went on holiday to Greece. We took a taxi to the airport early in the morning. Six hours later, we arrived in Athens. The sun was shining and it was very hot.

Mum was tired, so she stayed at the hotel. Dad and I were hungry, so we found a restaurant and tried the local food. I don't usually like fish, but the fish at this restaurant was delicious! Dad had a salad with cheese and tomatoes and lots of bread.

The next day we went on a guided tour of Athens. Then we met some Greek friends and explored the city together. In the evening we had dinner, listened to music and danced.

On the third day, we went on a boat trip to a small island near Athens. I was looking at the sea when I saw dolphins! They were swimming near the boat and jumping out of the water. I loved the island. There aren't any cars there, so people walk everywhere or ride donkeys!

We stayed in Greece for one week and it was fantastic.

0 Amanda and her family went to the airport by *taxi*.

1 In Athens the sun was shining and it was _____.

2 Amanda and her dad went to a restaurant because _____.

3 Mr Clarke had lots of bread with his _____.

4 The Clarke family went on a _____ of Athens.

5 There aren't _____ on the island.

◯ / 5

5 Complete the email with the words in the box.

> battery broke charger go microwave ~~was~~

Hi Alex,

We had a terrible time last weekend! We went on a trip, but the weather **0** _was_ bad and we didn't **1** _____ hiking. The house didn't have electricity because there was a storm. There was no TV and we didn't cook our dinner in the **2** _____ oven. I didn't text you because I dropped my mobile phone and **3** _____ the screen. My laptop wasn't working because the **4** _____ was dead and I left my portable **5** _____ at home.

See you soon, I hope!

Mike

◯ / 5

Writing

6 Write 70–80 words about a weekend you didn't enjoy because something happened. Use these questions to help you.

1 Where were you?
2 Who was with you?
3 What were you doing when something happened?
4 What happened next?
5 What was the result and how did you feel?

_____
_____
_____
_____
_____
_____
_____
_____
_____
_____
_____

◯ / 5

Listening ◯ / 10	Communication ◯ / 5
Reading ◯ / 10	Writing ◯ / 5
	Your total score ◯ / 30

© Pearson Education Limited 2019 PHOTOCOPIABLE

Skills Test A

name ______________________ class ________

Listening

1 🔊 **6 Listen and tick the correct answer.**

0 What time is it?

a ☑ 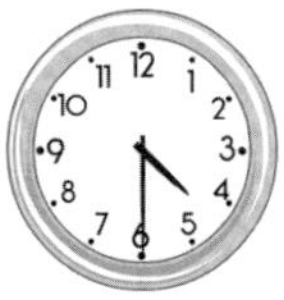
b ☐ 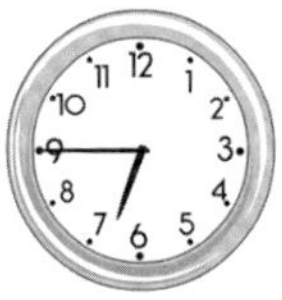
c ☐ 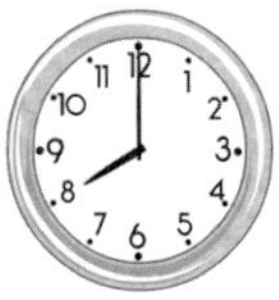

1 What does Emily's mum have to do first?

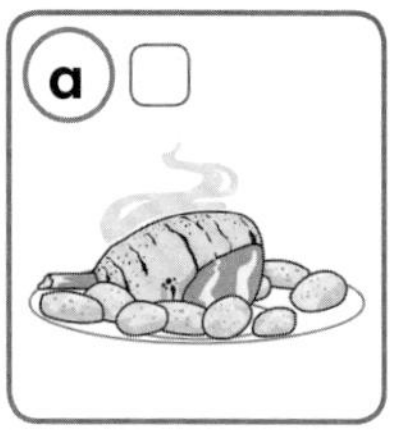
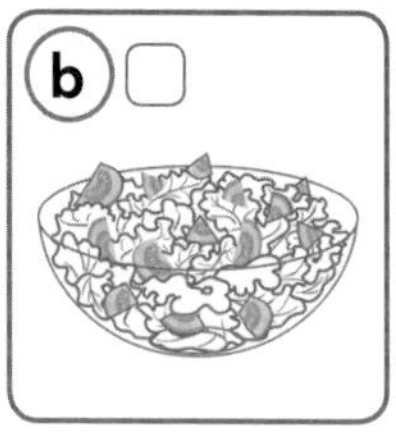
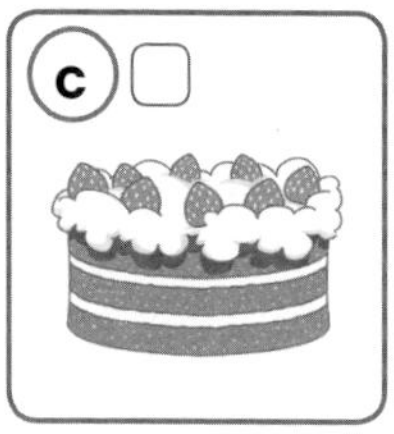

2 What should Emily do last?

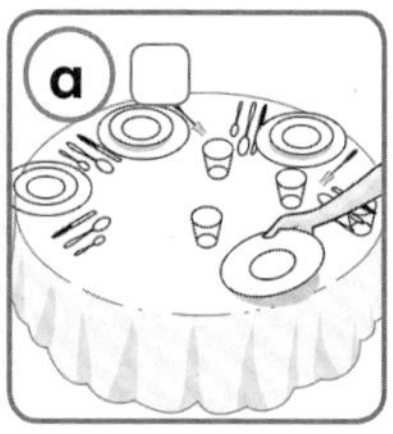
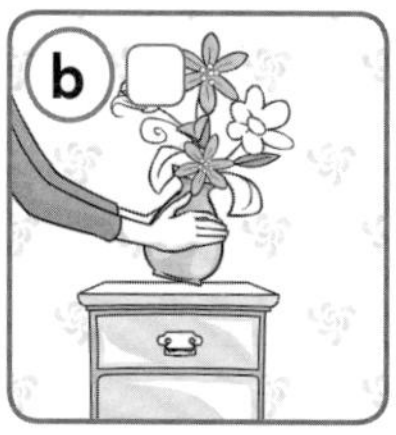
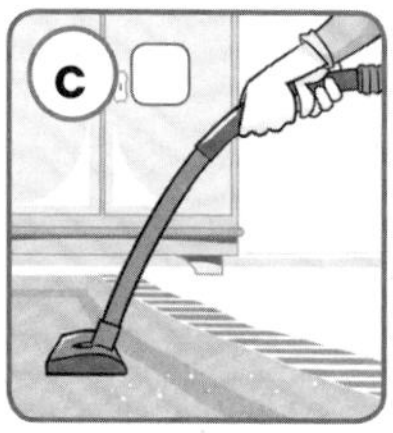

3 What has Emily's mum broken?

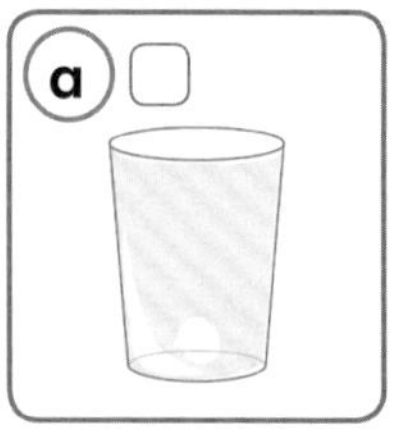
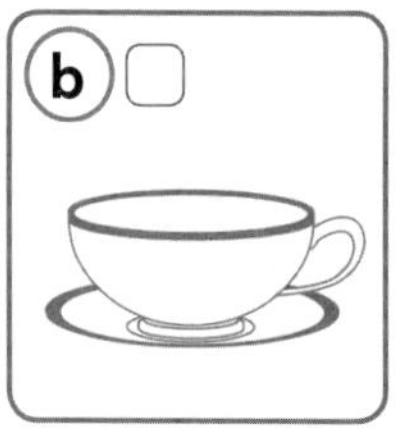
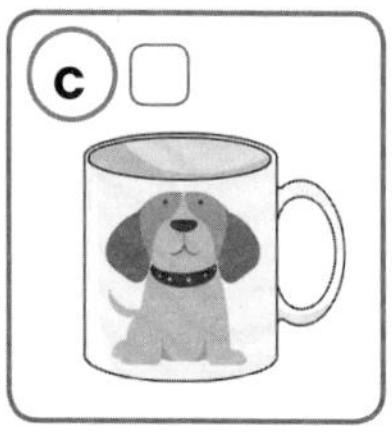

4 What ingredients does Emily have to buy?

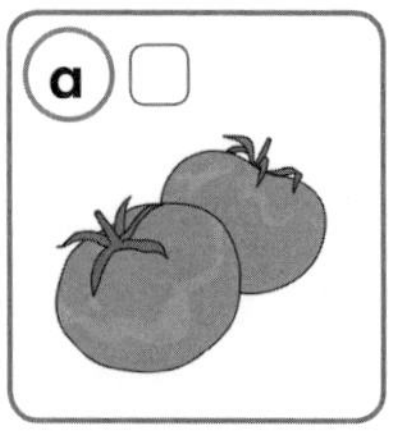
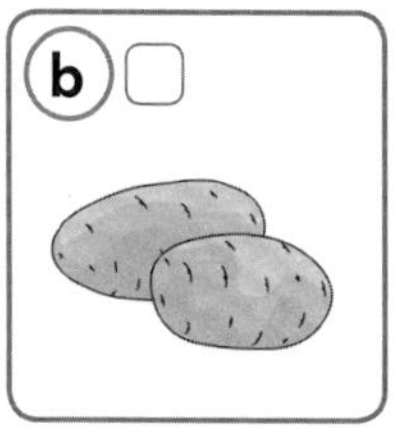
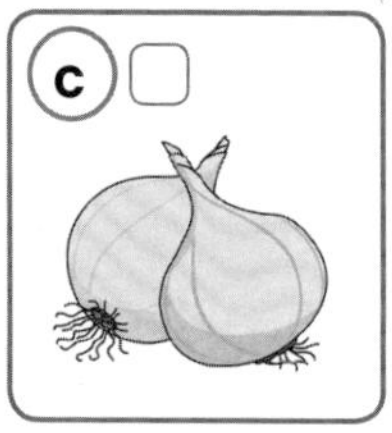

5 What has Emily's mum got on her hand?

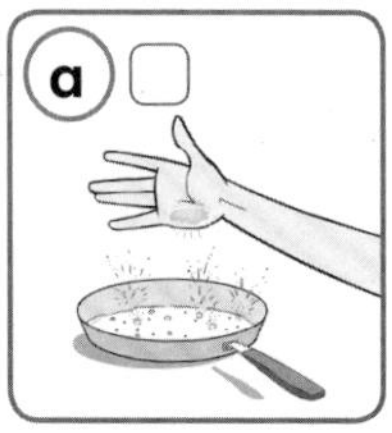
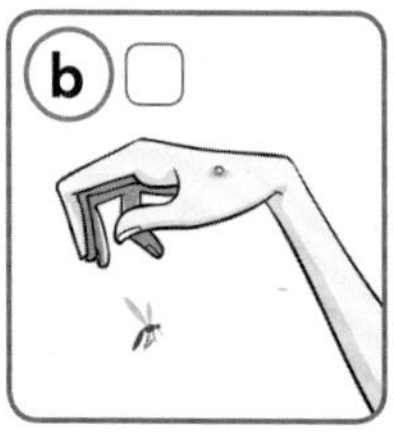
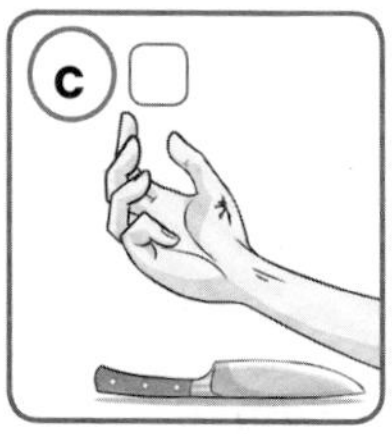

☐ / 5

2 🔊 **7 Listen and complete the recipe. Write one word or a number in each gap.**

FRENCH TOAST

0 _3_ eggs
1 ½ cups of 1 ________
salt
sugar
butter
bread

First beat the eggs and milk in a bowl.
2 ________ a little salt. Then slice the bread. You need 3 ________ pieces of bread for this recipe.
Put the bread in the bowl with the eggs and milk.
Then put some butter in a frying pan. Fry the bread for 4 ________ minutes on each side.
Put some 5 ________ on the bread. Fry each side again for about 15 seconds.
Serve with jam, honey or fruit.

☐ / 5

Communication

3 **Greg's friend Ian asks him some questions. Read Greg's answers and write Ian's questions.**

Ian: 0 _What's the matter?_

Greg: I've got a headache. I think I've got a temperature too.

Ian: 1 ______________________

Greg: Yes, you're right. I can lie down on the sofa.

Ian: 2 ______________________

Greg: No, I haven't seen the doctor.

Ian: 3 ______________________

Greg: Yes. I'd like some tea very much.

Ian: 4 ______________________

Greg: No, I don't want to take a painkiller.

Ian: 5 ______________________

Greg: No, I don't have to do any homework tonight.

☐ / 5

PHOTOCOPIABLE © Pearson Education Limited 2019

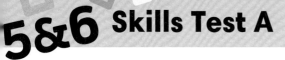

5&6 Skills Test A

name ______________________ class ________

Reading

4 Read Marion's email and answer the questions.

Hi Mike,

I've had a bad week. Poor Mum is ill. She's got the flu and she feels terrible. She had a temperature again today. She coughs all night and she's got a sore throat. I make her hot tea and orange juice so she can get well soon. Dad is feeling bad too. He hasn't got the flu, but he ate too much yesterday and now he's got a stomachache. And that's not all. My brother Jon has broken his arm. He was skateboarding with his friends when it happened. I'm sure he was doing something silly! So Mum is in bed, Dad is lying on the sofa in the living room and Jon is looking for painkillers.

It's seven o'clock now and I have to make dinner for me and Jon. Mum and Dad are too ill to cook. I've made some mint tea for Dad because he shouldn't eat anything today. Mum's had some tomato soup and toast. I've boiled some spaghetti and I've made tomato sauce for me and Jon. And after dinner I'm going to bed. I've got a headache!

Bye for now.

Marion

0 What's wrong with Marion's mum?
She's got the flu.

1 What does she do at night?
____

2 How did Marion's dad get sick?
____

3 What has happened to John?
____

4 Where is Marion's mum now?
____

5 What has Marion made for her dad?
____

☐ / [5]

5 Complete the text with the words in the box.

~~ever~~ have mix oven should tin

Have you [0] *ever* baked a cake? It isn't difficult. You [1] __________ to read the recipe carefully before you start and you [2] __________ have all the ingredients. It's also important to have the right size cake [3] __________. And don't forget: always [4] __________ the ingredients well and turn on the [5] __________ before you put the cake in it!

☐ / [5]

Writing

6 Give advice about what to do and what not to do when you have the flu. Write 60–70 words. Use these questions to help you.

1 How do you know that you have the flu?
2 What should you do?
3 What should you eat and drink?
4 What shouldn't you do?

____
____
____
____
____
____
____
____
____
____
____
____
____
____

☐ / [5]

Listening	☐ / [10]	Communication	☐ / [5]
Reading	☐ / [10]	Writing	☐ / [5]
		Your total score	☐ / [30]

© Pearson Education Limited 2019 PHOTOCOPIABLE

name _____ class _____

Listening

1 **6** Listen and tick the correct answer.

0 What time is it?

c ☑

b ☐

c ☐

1 What does Emily's mum have to do first?

a ☐

b ☐
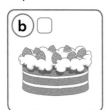

c ☐

2 What should Emily do last?

a ☐

b ☐

c ☐

3 What has Emily's mum broken?

a ☐

b ☐

c ☐

4 What ingredients does Emily have to buy?

a ☐

b ☐

c ☐
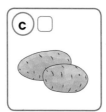

5 What has Emily's mum got on her hand?

a ☐

b ☐

c ☐

☐ / 5

2 **7** Listen and complete the recipe. Write one word or a number in each gap.

FRENCH TOAST

0 3 eggs
1 ½ cups of **1** _____
salt
sugar
butter
2 _____

First beat the eggs and milk in a bowl. Add a little salt. Then **3** _____ the bread. You need eight pieces of bread for this recipe. Put the bread in the bowl with the eggs and milk. Then put some butter in the frying pan. Fry the bread for **4** _____ minutes on each side. Then put some sugar on the bread. Fry again for **5** _____ seconds on each side.
When ready, serve with jam, honey or fruit.

☐ / 5

Communication

3 Greg's friend Ian asks him some questions. Read Greg's answers and write Ian's questions.

Jeremy: **0** *What's the matter?*

Tom: I don't feel very well. I've got earache and a sore throat.

Jeremy: **1** _____

Tom: No, I don't want to take a painkiller.

Jeremy: **2** _____

Tom: No, I haven't seen the doctor.

Jeremy: **3** _____

Tom: Yes, that's a good idea. I'd like some tea with lemon and honey.

Jeremy: **4** _____

Tom: Yes, I would like to lie down.

Jeremy: **5** _____

Tom: No, I don't have to get up early tomorrow.

☐ / 5

© Pearson Education Limited 2019 PHOTOCOPIABLE

5&6 Skills Test B

name ____________________ class ________

Reading

4 Read Marion's email and answer the questions.

Hi Mike,

I've had a bad week. Poor Mum is ill. She's got the flu and she feels terrible. She had a temperature again today. She coughs all night and she's got a sore throat. I make her hot tea and orange juice so she can get well soon. Dad is feeling bad too. He hasn't got the flu, but he ate too much yesterday and now he's got a stomachache. And that's not all. My brother Jon has broken his arm. He was skateboarding with his friends when it happened. I'm sure he was doing something silly! So Mum is in bed, Dad is lying on the sofa in the living room and Jon is looking for painkillers.

It's seven o'clock now and I have to make dinner for me and Jon. Mum and Dad are too ill to cook. I've made some mint tea for Dad because he shouldn't eat anything today. Mum's had some tomato soup and toast. I've boiled some spaghetti and I've made tomato sauce for me and Jon. And after dinner I'm going to bed. I've got a headache!

Bye for now.

Marion

0 What's wrong with Marion's mum?
She's got the flu.

1 What does she drink?
____

2 When did Marion's dad eat too much?
____

3 What was Jon doing when he broke his arm?
____

4 Where is Marion's dad now?
____

5 What are Marion and Jon having for dinner?
____

[ ] / [5]

5 Complete the text with the words in the box.

bake ~~ever~~ have oven should tin

Have you [0]*ever* made an apple pie? It isn't difficult. You [1]__________ to use good apples and the right size cake [2]__________. You [3]__________ always read the recipe carefully before you start. And don't forget to turn on the [4]__________ before you put the pie in it. [5]__________ the pie for about 30 minutes, until it is brown.

[ ] / [5]

Writing

6 Give advice about what to do and what not to do when you have the flu. Write 60–70 words. Use these questions to help you.

1 How do you know that you have the flu?
2 What should you do?
3 What should you eat and drink?
4 What shouldn't you do?

____

[ ] / [5]

Listening	[ ] / [10]	Communication	[ ] / [5]
Reading	[ ] / [10]	Writing	[ ] / [5]
		Your total score	[ ] / [30]

© Pearson Education Limited 2019 PHOTOCOPIABLE

name _____ class _____

Listening

1 🔊 **8** Billy can't find some things and his sister Sue is helping him. Listen and write answers to questions 1–5.

0 What is Billy looking for?
A USB stick and a portable charger

1 Where did Sue find Billy's USB stick?

_____

2 Whose portable charger did Billy borrow?

_____

3 When was the last time Billy used Mum's USB stick?

_____

4 Did Billy stay on the balcony for a long time?

_____

5 Why did Billy go to the kitchen?

_____

☐ / 5

2 🔊 **9** Listen to Becky talking about her neighbourhood. Write T (true) or F (false).

0 Becky lives in a block of flats. ☐ T
1 All the balconies looked nice. ☐
2 People planted flowers in the garden. ☐
3 Becky's balcony is too small for a tree. ☐
4 The chairs on the balconies cost a lot of money. ☐
5 The balconies are very close together. ☐

☐ / 5

Communication

3 Look at the pictures. Put the sentences in the dialogue in the correct order. There is one extra sentence.

a ☐ Do you need any help with your chores?
b ☐ Yes, I'd love to. I love burgers!
c ☐ You make the best burgers, Mr Brown.
d ☐ 1 Do you want to go to the beach on Saturday?
e ☐ I'm sorry, I can't. I have to do my chores on Saturday.
f ☐ That's true, Dad. They're fantastic.
g ☐ How about Sunday. We're having a barbecue. Would you like to come?

☐ / 5

© Pearson Education Limited 2019 | PHOTOCOPIABLE

name ______________________ class ________

Reading

4 Read the blog post. Complete the sentences with one, two or three words.

HOME | ABOUT ME | CONTACT

My New Home

by Beverley Symons

First, the good news: Mum's starting her new job next month! She's happy because she really wanted it. Then the sad news: we're moving because Mum's job is in the country. Dad doesn't mind because he will work from home on his computer, but I'll miss our semi-detached house in Birmingham.

Some people don't like living in semi-detached houses, but we don't have any problems with our neighbours. My bedroom is next to their daughter's bedroom. I can hear her sometimes and she can hear me, but it doesn't matter.

Tomorrow we're packing our things. We aren't taking all our furniture because our new home is a cottage and it's smaller than this house.

Our cottage is near Harris Hall. Harris Hall was the house of a rich family. It had 64 bedrooms and lots of stairs. Now it's a hotel. It still has lots of stairs but lifts too! There's a restaurant on the ground floor and Mum is the new chef there!

Next week we're driving to a town near Harris Hall. We want to check it out and see what activities we can do there. My new school is in the town too.

I hope we'll be happy there. I'll write all about it soon!

0 Beverley has some good news and some *sad news*.

1 Beverley's dad will work ______________ on his computer.

2 Beverley's bedroom is ______________ her neighbours' daughter's bedroom.

3 Beverley's new home is a ______________.

4 The hotel has a restaurant on ______________.

5 Beverly and her parents ______________ to a town near Harris Hall next week.

[ ] / 5

5 Complete the text with the words in the box.

call foreign late ~~polite~~ shake turn

Good manners are important

It's important to be [0]*polite*, especially because so many people today think it's all right to be rude.

- [1]__________ hands when you meet people. Look at them and smile.
- When you arrange to meet someone, don't be [2]__________. It's not very nice.
- Don't interrupt people. Wait your [3]__________ before you say or do something.
- Learn a [4]__________ language: people love it when you speak to them in their own language – and it doesn't matter if you make mistakes!
- Be kind. [5]__________ your grandparents often, especially if they live on their own.

[ ] / 5

Writing

6 Write 70–80 words about your predictions for the future. Use these questions to help you.

1 What will you do when you finish school?
2 Where will you live?
2 What will your best friend do in the future?
4 Will you travel to other countries?
5 How will you change?

____
____
____
____
____
____
____
____
____
____

[ ] / 5

Listening	[ ] / 10	Communication	[ ] / 5
Reading	[ ] / 10	Writing	[ ] / 5
		Your total score	[ ] / 30

© Pearson Education Limited 2019 PHOTOCOPIABLE

name _____ class _____

Listening

1 🔊 **8** Billy can't find some things and his sister Sue is helping him. Listen and write answers to questions 1–5.

0 What is Billy looking for?
A USB stick and a portable charger

1 Where did Sue find Billy's portable charger?
_____

2 Whose USB stick did Billy borrow?
_____

3 When was the last time Billy used Dad's portable charger?
_____

4 How long did Billy stay on the balcony?
_____

5 Did Billy go to the kitchen to eat something?
_____

☐ / 5

2 🔊 **9** Listen to Becky talking about her neighbourhood. Write T (true) or F (false).

0 Becky lives in a block of flats. | T |
1 People cleaned up their flats. | ☐ |
2 All people planted trees on their balconies. | ☐ |
3 Becky wants birds to come to her balcony. | ☐ |
4 The chairs on the balconies aren't new. | ☐ |
5 The balcony party is next week. | ☐ |

☐ / 5

Communication

3 Look at the pictures. Put the sentences in the dialogue in the correct order. There is one extra sentence.

a ☐ You make the best burgers, Mr Jones.
b [1] Do you want to go to the beach on Saturday?
c ☐ Yes, I'd love to. I love burgers!
d ☐ I'm sorry, I can't. I have to do my chores on Saturday.
e ☐ Do you need any help with your chores?
f ☐ What about Sunday? We're having a barbecue. Would you like to come?
g ☐ That's true, Dad. They're fantastic.

☐ / 5

© Pearson Education Limited 2019 | PHOTOCOPIABLE

name ______________________ class ________

Reading

4 Read the blog post. Complete the sentences with one, two or three words.

HOME | ABOUT ME | CONTACT

My New Home

by Beverley Symons

First, the good news: Mum's starting her new job next month! She's happy because she really wanted it. Then the sad news: we're moving because Mum's job is in the country. Dad doesn't mind because he will work from home on his computer, but I'll miss our semi-detached house in Birmingham.

Some people don't like living in semi-detached houses, but we don't have any problems with our neighbours. My bedroom is next to their daughter's bedroom. I can hear her sometimes and she can hear me, but it doesn't matter.

Tomorrow we're packing our things. We aren't taking all our furniture because our new home is a cottage and it's smaller than this house.

Our cottage is near Harris Hall. Harris Hall was the house of a rich family. It had 64 bedrooms and lots of stairs. Now it's a hotel. It still has lots of stairs but lifts too! There's a restaurant on the ground floor and Mum is the new chef there!

Next week we're driving to a town near Harris Hall. We want to check it out and see what activities we can do there. My new school is in the town too.

I hope we'll be happy there. I'll write all about it soon!

0 Beverley has some good news and some *sad news*.
1 Beverley's dad will work from home on ______________ .
2 Beverley lives in a ______________ house now.
3 Beverley and her parents are ______________ ______________ tomorrow.
4 There is a restaurant on ______________ of the hotel.
5 Beverley's new ______________ is in a town near Harris Hall.

[ ] / [5]

5 Complete the text with the words in the box.

foreign interrupt late ~~polite~~ shake visit

Good manners are important

It's important to be [0]*polite*, especially because so many people today think it's all right to be rude.

- When you meet people, [1]__________ hands. Look at them and smile.
- Be kind. [2]__________ your grandparents often. Especially if they live on their own.
- Don't be [3]__________ when you arrange to meet someone. It's not nice at all.
- Don't [4]__________ people when they are talking. Wait your turn.
- Learn a [5]__________ language: people love it when you speak to them in their own language – and it doesn't matter if you make mistakes!

[ ] / [5]

Writing

6 Write 70–80 words about your predictions for the future. Use these questions to help you.

1 What will you do when you finish school?
2 Where will you live?
2 What will your best friend do in the future?
4 Will you travel to other countries?
5 How will you change?

____
____
____
____
____
____
____
____
____
____

[ ] / [5]

Listening	[ ] / [10]	Communication	[ ] / [5]
Reading	[ ] / [10]	Writing	[ ] / [5]
		Your total score	[ ] / [30]

© Pearson Education Limited 2019 [PHOTOCOPIABLE]

1–4 Mid-Year Test A

name ______________________ class ________

Vocabulary

1 Circle the correct answer.

Kids, please don't forget to do the chores!
– [0]*Load* / *Set* the dishwasher after breakfast.
– [1]*Iron* / *Hang* out the washing in the garden.
– We need some things from the supermarket. The shopping [2]*list* / *note* is on the table.
- [3]*Check* / *Pay* the prices before you buy things, and don't buy the most expensive ones!
- Don't buy the bread from the supermarket. Go to the [4]*chemist's* / *baker's*.
- And go to the [5]*greengrocer's* / *newsagent's* for the potatoes and fruit.

[ ] / 5

2 Complete the text with the words in the box.

boat bored get ~~guided~~ hiking messy

Dear Angela,
I have a problem. I don't like going on holiday with my family. My parents love going on [0]*guided* tours or [1]__________ in the mountains. I don't. We walk for hours and I [2]__________ tired. My brother wants to do different things all the time because he gets [3]__________ easily. He wants to do water sports, go on [4]__________ trips, go cycling … I just want to sit on the beach quietly. My sister and I share a hotel room, but she's [5]__________. She leaves her clothes on the floor. It's terrible! What can I do?
Emma

[ ] / 5

3 Complete the text.

My favourite thing? It's my smartphone. I [0]**t**u r**n** it on when I get up in the morning and off only when I go to bed. I've got lots of useful [1]**a** _ _ **s** on it and I download new ones every month. I change the [2]**r** _ _ _ _ _ _ **e** of my phone every week. I always carry my portable [3]**c** _ _ _ _ _ **r** with me because I don't want the battery to die. Another thing I like is the [4]**r** _ _ _ _ **e** control for our smart TV. Once we lost it and it was terrible! And of course, I love my games [5]**c** _ _ _ _ _ **e**. I spend a lot of time playing computer games!

[ ] / 5

Grammar

4 Complete the text with the Present Simple or the Present Continuous form of the verbs.

I like shopping. I [0] *go* (go) to the shopping centre every Saturday. Right now, I [1]__________ (look) at some jeans in a clothes shop. I also [2]__________ (need) a new jacket. My sister is at the shopping centre too. She [3]__________ (not like) clothes shops, so at the moment she [4]__________ (wait) for me at a café. What about you? [5]__________ (you / spend) a lot of time in shops?

[ ] / 5

5 Complete the sentences with the correct form of the adjective in brackets.

0 A microwave oven is *more useful* (useful) than a blender.
1 I think this is __________ (funny) programme on TV.
2 I'm not as __________ (organised) as him.
3 This smartphone is __________ (good) than that one.
4 I don't like this bag. It isn't __________ (big) enough.
5 This is __________ (stylish) coat in the shop.

[ ] / 5

6 Circle the correct answer.

0 Where *was* / *were* you yesterday at four o'clock?
1 We *come* / *came* home late last night.
2 *Was* / *Did* Bill finish his homework early yesterday?
3 What was John *do* / *doing* last night at eight o'clock?
4 Mary *looked* / *was* looking for a new dress when I saw her.
5 The children didn't *have* / *had* a good time at the beach because it was too hot.

[ ] / 5

Vocabulary [ ] / 15	Grammar [ ] / 15
	Your total score [ ] / 30

PHOTOCOPIABLE © Pearson Education Limited 2019

name _____

class _____

Listening

7 🔊 **10** Listen to Linda and her big brother Adam and complete the sentences. Use one or two words or a number.

0 Adam tells Linda to *put away* her clothes.

1 Linda thinks Adam is very _____.

2 Linda didn't make _____ yesterday.

3 Linda lost her _____ in Italy.

4 USB sticks cost £ _____ this week.

5 Linda can't pay _____ because she doesn't have enough money.

6 The newsagent's is next to the _____ .

☐ / ⑥

Communication

8 Complete the dialogues with the words and phrases in the box.

> a shame   busy   can I   could you
> here you are   ~~no problem~~   that's fine
> upset   what size

0 A: Can you open the door for me, please?
   B: *No problem*.

1 A: Do you need any help with that box? It's very heavy!
   B: No, _____, thank you.

2 A: _____ help you?
   B: No, thanks, I'm just looking.

3 A: _____ are you?
   B: Medium, I think.

4 A: Do you have these shoes in black?
   B: Yes, we do. _____ .

5 A: _____ drive me to the park, please?
   B: Not now, sorry. I'm _____ .

6 A: You look _____ . What happened?
   B: I didn't pass my Maths test.
   A: That's _____ .

☐ / ⑧

Reading

9 Read Matt's blog post about his holiday and circle T (true) or F (false).

🗕   ↻

Our holiday
by Matt Atkinson

We didn't go on holiday last August because Dad had too much work. We stayed at home. We sometimes visited Granny and Grandad in the country at the weekend.

Then one evening, we were sitting near the fire. It was cold and dark. Suddenly, Dad said to Mum: 'We didn't have a summer holiday. Let's go to a warm country for ten days!' 'That's a wonderful idea!' said Mum. So we bought tickets to Jamaica!

We arrived there late on Saturday night and took a taxi to our hotel. It had a big swimming pool and the beach was a hundred metres away.

The next day, Mum and I went snorkelling. We were swimming in the warm water when we saw some dolphins. Dad and my sister stayed at the hotel. They swam in the pool and read books all day.

We did other things too. We went sightseeing, and in the evening we listened to reggae – that's Jamaican music. It was too hot to go hiking in the Blue Mountains, but we went on a boat trip on the Martha Brae River. Our guide was a friendly man and he told us about the animals and birds we saw.

It was the best holiday of my life!

0 Matt stayed at home last August because his dad had too much work.   Ⓣ/ F

1 He never visited his grandparents.   T / F

2 Matt's grandparents live in the country.   T / F

3 The holiday in a warm country was Mum's idea.   T / F

4 Matt and his family arrived in Jamaica at the weekend.   T / F

5 Matt and his mum saw dolphins one day.   T / F

6 Matt and his family went hiking in Jamaica.   T / F

☐ / ⑥

© Pearson Education Limited 2019

PHOTOCOPIABLE

Listening ☐ / ⑥	Communication	☐ / ⑧
Reading ☐ / ⑥	**Your total score**	☐ / ⑳

1–4 Mid-Year Test B

name ______________________ class ________

Vocabulary

1 Circle the correct answer.

Kids, please don't forget to do the chores!
– [0] Load / Set the dishwasher after breakfast.
– [1] *Hang / Put* away the clean clothes in your rooms.
– We need some things from the supermarket.
Take the big shopping [2] *bag / queue* with you.
- There's some money on the kitchen table. Don't forget to get a [3] *cashier / receipt* for the things.
- Don't buy the fruit from the supermarket. Go to the [4] *greengrocer's / chemist's*.
- And go to the [5] *newsagent's / baker's* for the bread.

☐ / 5

2 Complete the text with the words in the box.

bored explore get guided ~~tidy~~ trips

Dear Nina,
I have a problem. I don't like going on holiday with my family. My sister and I share a hotel room, but she isn't [0] *tidy*. I hate it when she leaves her clothes on the floor. My brother gets [1] ____________ easily, so he wants to do different things all the time. He wants to go on boat [2] ____________, go cycling, go hiking … He wants to [3] ____________ the area, but I don't. I [4] ____________ lost easily. My parents love going on [5] ____________ tours and I want to relax on holiday. What can I do?
Tessa

☐ / 5

3 Complete the text.

My favourite thing? It's my smartphone. I [0] **t** *u r* **n** it on when I get up in the morning and off only when I go to bed. I always have my portable [1] **c** _ _ _ _ _ **r** with me because I don't want the battery to die. I change the [2] **r** _ _ _ _ _ _ **e** of my phone every week. I've got lots of useful [3] **a** _ _ **s** on it and I download new ones every month. I also like my games [4] **c** _ _ _ _ _ **e**. I spend a lot of time playing computer games! Another thing I like is the [5] **r** _ _ _ _ **e** control for our smart TV. Once we lost it and it was terrible!

☐ / 5

Grammar

4 Complete the text with the Present Simple or the Present Continuous form of the verbs.

I like shopping. I [0] *go* (go) to the shopping centre every Saturday. I [1] ____________ (want) some new clothes for the summer, and right now I [2] ____________ (try) on a pair of jeans in a clothes shop. My friend is at the shopping centre too. He [3] ____________ (not need) any new clothes, so at the moment he [4] ____________ (wait) for me at a café. What about you? [5] ____________ (you / spend) a lot of time in shops?

☐ / 5

5 Complete the sentences with the correct form of the adjective in brackets.

0 A microwave oven is *more useful* (useful) than a blender.
1 Your problem is ____________ (bad) than my problem.
2 Today is ____________ (happy) day of my life.
3 This is ____________ (stylish) bag in the shop.
4 He can't buy that hat. It isn't ____________ (big) enough.
5 They aren't as ____________ (patient) as her.

☐ / 5

6 Circle the correct answer.

0 Where was / *were* you yesterday at four o'clock?
1 We *get / got* up very early yesterday morning.
2 What was Jack *do / doing* last night at seven o'clock?
3 *Was / Did* Emma come home late last night?
4 The children didn't *play / played* volleyball at the beach because it was too hot.
5 Julia *bought / was buying* a new coat when I saw her.

☐ / 5

Vocabulary ☐ / 15 Grammar ☐ / 15
Your total score ☐ / 30

PHOTOCOPIABLE © Pearson Education Limited 2019

name   class

Listening

7 🔊 10 Listen to Linda and her big brother Adam and complete the sentences. Use one or two words or a number.

0 Adam tells Linda to *put away* her clothes.
1 Adam thinks Linda is very _____.
2 Linda went _____ with her class.
3 Linda needs a new _____.
4 USB sticks were £_____, but now they are on special offer.
5 Linda can't pay _____ because she doesn't know where it is.
6 The newspaper is for _____.

☐ / ⑥

Communication

8 Complete the dialogues with the words and phrases in the box.

> busy   can I   could you   do you need
> here you are   look   ~~no problem~~
> to hear that   what size

0 A: Can you open the door for me, please?
  B: *No problem*.
1 A: _____ are you?
  B: I think I'm a small.
2 A: _____ help me with my homework, please?
  B: Not now, sorry. I'm _____.
3 A: _____ any help with your chores?
  B: Yes, please.
4 A: What's wrong? You _____ upset.
  B: I lost my phone.
  A: I'm sorry _____.
5 A: _____ help you?
  B: No, thanks, I'm just looking.
6 A: Do you have this coat in brown?
  B: Yes, we do. _____.

☐ / ⑧

Reading

9 Read Matt's blog post about his holiday and circle T (true) or F (false).

Our holiday
by Matt Atkinson

We didn't go on holiday last August because Dad had too much work. We stayed at home. We sometimes visited Granny and Grandad in the country at the weekend.

Then one evening, we were sitting near the fire. It was cold and dark. Suddenly, Dad said to Mum: 'We didn't have a summer holiday. Let's go to a warm country for ten days!' 'That's a wonderful idea!' said Mum. So we bought tickets to Jamaica!

We arrived there late on Saturday night and took a taxi to our hotel. It had a big swimming pool and the beach was a hundred metres away.

The next day, Mum and I went snorkelling. We were swimming in the warm water when we saw some dolphins. Dad and my sister stayed at the hotel. They swam in the pool and read books all day.

We did other things too. We went sightseeing and in the evening we listened to reggae – that's Jamaican music. It was too hot to go hiking, but we went on a boat trip on the Martha Brae River. Our guide was a friendly man and he told us about the animals and birds we saw.

It was the best holiday of my life!

0 Matt stayed at home last August because his dad had too much work. (T)/ F
1 He sometimes visited his grandparents. T / F
2 Matt's grandparents live in a town. T / F
3 Matt and his family went to Jamaica for two weeks. T / F
4 There was a big swimming pool in the hotel. T / F
5 Matt's dad and sister spent the second day on the beach. T / F
6 Matt and his family saw some wild animals and birds. T / F

☐ / ⑥

© Pearson Education Limited 2019 PHOTOCOPIABLE

| Listening ☐ / ⑥ | Communication ☐ / ⑧ |
| Reading ☐ / ⑥ | **Your total score** ☐ / ⑳ |

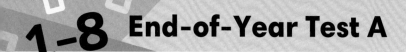

_____   _____
name   class

Vocabulary

1 Complete the text with the words in the box.

business ~~cottage~~ out shake village water

HOME SWEET HOME
by Helen Todd

My family and I live in a **⁰**_cottage_ in a small
¹_____ in Yorkshire. My parents have
their own **²**_____ here and my brother
and I go to the local school.
People here are very friendly. They smile, say
good morning and **³**_____ hands
when they meet in the street. They chat to their
neighbours when they **⁴**_____ the
plants in the garden or take **⁵**_____ the
rubbish. It's a great place to live.

☐ / 5

2 Circle the correct answer.

The best **⁰**_baker's_/ _newsagent's_ in town is The Pie
Shop. People stand in a **¹**_queue_ / _cashier_ to buy
bread and apple pies from there. Tourists come
to **²**_check_ / _try_ the local food – our area is famous
for apple pies! Mrs Taylor, the owner, makes the
bread and pies. When they come out of the **³**_pot_ /
oven, they smell delicious! Mrs Taylor's son and
daughter also work at The Pie Shop. They **⁴**_peel_ /
beat and chop the apples, serve the customers
and clean **⁵**_away_ / _up_ the kitchen every evening.

☐ / 5

3 Complete the sentences.

0 When it gets **d** a r **k**, we turn on the lights.
1 I plugged in the **b**_ _ _ _ _**r** and made
  a smoothie with yoghurt and fruit.
2 Please put the dirty plates, knives, **f**_ _ _ _**s**
  and spoons in the dishwasher.
3 I washed the bowl in the kitchen **s**_ _ _**k**.
4 Listen! That's your phone. My phone has
  a different **r**_ _ _ _ _ _**e**.
5 He put his clean socks away in a **d**_ _ _ _**r**.

☐ / 5

Grammar

4 Circle the correct answer.

0 What time _does Jim get_/ _is Jim getting_ up every
  morning?
1 Dad _leaves_ / _left_ the office a few minutes ago.
2 I _try_ / _I'm trying_ to do this exercise, but I don't
  understand it.
3 I can't come with you tomorrow. _I play_ /
  I'm playing tennis with Paula.
4 She _didn't water_ / _doesn't water_ the plants
  yesterday, so please water them now.
5 We _were exploring_ / _explored_ the old town
  when we got lost.

☐ / 5

**5 Complete the sentences with the correct form
of the verbs. Use _will_ or the Present Perfect.**

0 I'm hungry because I _haven't had_ (not have)
  breakfast.
1 '_____ (you / ever / stay)
  in a hotel?' 'No, I haven't.'
2 Max loves animals. I think he _____
  (be) a vet one day.
3 Oh, no! I _____ (break) my favorite
  mug.
4 Jim _____ (make) spaghetti. Try it, it's
  delicious.
5 What _____ (you / do) in the future?

☐ / 5

6 Circle the correct answer.

0 Dad is 40 and Mum is two years _younger_/
  the youngest than him. She's 38.
1 I can't play basketball. I'm not _tall enough_ /
  too tall.
2 He always listens _careful_ / _carefully_ to his
  teachers.
3 Do we _have to_ / _should_ ask for permission?
4 I _can_ / _mustn't_ be late! Mum will be angry.
5 That's the _worse_ / _worst_ programme on TV.

☐ / 5

Vocabulary ☐ / 15   Grammar ☐ / 15
                     Your total score ☐ / 30

© Pearson Education Limited 2019 | PHOTOCOPIABLE

1-8 End-of-Year Test A

name _____ class _____

Listening

Reading

7 🔊 **11 Listen to five people talking about health problems. Circle T (true) or F (false).**

0 Ben always goes to see the doctor when he gets earache. T /Ⓕ
1 Ben doesn't want to stop snorkelling. T / F
2 Molly got headaches, because her eyes got tired. T / F
3 Molly wears glasses now. T / F
4 Duncan got the flu eight months ago. T / F
5 Olivia's dad put cold tea on her mosquito bites. T / F
6 Spicy food is bad for Stuart's stomach. T / F

☐ / ⑥

Communication

8 Complete the dialogues. Match 1–8 with a–h.

0 A: Can you help me with the cooking, please?
  B: _i_
1 A: Would you like to watch a DVD or listen to music?
  B: ____
2 A: Can I use the tablet?
  B: ____
3 A: Do you have this in red?
  B: ____
4 A: Are you free on Saturday afternoon? Would you like to hang out?
  B: ____
5 A: I think this singer is great. What do you think?
  B: ____
6 A: Can I help you?
  B: ____
7 A: I think you should lie down.
  B: ____
8 A: What happened?
  B: ____

a I agree with you.
b I don't mind. You choose.
c I fell and that's why I've got all these bruises.
d Yes, you're right. I really don't feel well.
e No, thanks, I'm just looking.
f Sorry, we don't.
g Sorry, you can't. I'm online right now.
h That sounds fun. Thank you.
i No problem.

☐ / ⑧

9 Read the article and complete the sentences with one word.

Make the world a better place

Small actions can make the world better.

Start with your family
❖ Do some chores: hang out the washing or take out the rubbish. Your mum and dad will be happy.
❖ Give your parents a big hug and say you love them to make them feel good.

Do something nice for other people
❖ Invite new neighbours to your home. Make them feel welcome.
❖ Collect money and food for charity that helps poor people.

Do something for your neighbourhood too
❖ Clean up the streets with your friends so your neighbourhood can look nice.
❖ Plant trees and flowers in the park to make it more beautiful.

0 Small actions can make the world _better_.
1 Your parents will be happy when you do some _____.
2 Your parents will feel good when you give them a big _____.
3 Make new neighbours feel welcome – _____ them to your home.
4 You can collect food and _____ to help poor people.
5 Your _____ can be nice when you clean up the streets.
6 More flowers and trees can make the _____ beautiful.

☐ / ⑥

Listening ☐ / ⑥   Communication ☐ / ⑧
Reading ☐ / ⑥   **Your total score** ☐ / ⑳

© Pearson Education Limited 2019 PHOTOCOPIABLE

73

1–8 End-of-Year Test B

name _______________ class _______

Vocabulary

1 Complete the text with the words in the box.

~~cottage~~ hang own rubbish shake village

HOME SWEET HOME

by Nigel Barnes

My family and I live in a [0]*cottage* in a small [1]_______________ in Yorkshire. My parents have their [2]_______________ business here and my brother and I go to the local school.

People here are very friendly. They chat to their neighbours when they [3]_______________ out the washing in the garden or take out the [4]_______________. They smile, say good morning and [5]_______________ hands when they meet in the street. It's a great place to live.

[ ] / 5

2 Circle the correct answer.

The best [0]*baker's / newsagent's* in town is The Pie Shop. Mr Henley, the owner, makes the bread and pies. When they come out of the [1]*oven / pot*, they smell delicious! Mr Henley's daughters help him at the shop. They [2]*beat / peel* and chop the apples for the pies and serve the customers. They also clean [3]*up / away* the kitchen every evening. People stand in a [4]*cashier / queue* to buy bread from The Pie Shop. Tourists come to [5]*try / check* the local food – our area is famous for apple pies!

[ ] / 5

3 Complete the sentences.

0 When it gets **d** *a* *r* **k**, we turn on the lights.
1 He looked at his face in the **m** _ _ _ _ **r** before he went out.
2 Please put your clean T-shirts away in a **d** _ _ _ _ **r**.
3 I put the dirty plates, knives, **s** _ _ _ _ **s** and forks in the dishwasher.
4 You can make a smoothie in the **b** _ _ _ _ _ **r** with fruit and milk.
5 I must charge my phone. The **b** _ _ _ _ _ **y** is 2%.

[ ] / 5

Grammar

4 Circle the correct answer.

0 What time *does Jim get / is Jim getting* up every morning?
1 *We meet / We're meeting* our friends at three o'clock tomorrow.
2 Ann *was waiting / waited* for a bus when I saw her.
3 Mum *goes / went* to France two years ago.
4 I *don't tidy / didn't tidy* my room last weekend, so I'm doing it now.
5 *They try / They're trying* to do the exercise, but they don't understand it.

[ ] / 5

5 Complete the sentences with the correct form of the verbs. Use *will* or the Present Perfect.

0 I'm hungry because I *haven't had* (not have) breakfast.
1 '_______________ (you / ever / visit) London?' 'No, I haven't.'
2 Oh, no! I _______________ (break) my favorite mug.
3 Amy loves painting. I think she _______________ (be) an artist one day.
4 Where _______________ (you / live) in the future?
5 Max _______________ (bake) a cake. Try it, it's delicious.

[ ] / 5

6 Circle the correct answer.

0 Dad is 40 and Mum is two years *younger / the youngest* than him. She's 38.
1 We don't *should / have to* go to school tomorrow.
2 That's the *funnier / funniest* programme on TV.
3 I can't carry that. I'm not *strong enough / too strong*.
4 She can sing very *good / well*.
5 Yes, you *can / mustn't* borrow my tablet. No problem.

[ ] / 5

Vocabulary [ ] / 15 Grammar [ ] / 15
Your total score [ ] / 30

© Pearson Education Limited 2019 PHOTOCOPIABLE

name   class

Listening

7 🔊 **11** Listen to five people talking about health problems. Circle T (true) or F (false).

0 Ben always goes to see the doctor when he gets earache.   T /Ⓕ

1 Ben has stopped snorkelling.   T / F

2 Molly doesn't get headaches now.   T / F

3 Duncan was ill for six days.   T / F

4 Duncan had to stay in bed.   T / F

5 Olivia's mum put lemon juice on her mosquito bites.   T / F

6 Stuart's granny thinks rice is good for a stomachache.   T / F

◯ / ⑥

Communication

8 Complete the dialogues. Match 1–8 with a–h.

0 A: Can you help me with the cooking, please?
 B: _i_

1 A: Do you have these in a medium?
 B: ____

2 A: This is a very funny programme. What do you think?
 B: ____

3 A: I think you should lie down.
 B: ____

4 A: Would you like to go cycling or swimming?
 B: ____

5 A: What happened?
 B: ____

6 A: Would you like to hang out on Friday?
 B: ____

7 A: Could I borrow your phone?
 B: ____

8 A: Can I help you?
 B: ____

 a I disagree with you.
 b No, thanks, I'm just looking.
 c Not now, sorry. I'm using it at the moment.
 d Yes, you're right. I really don't feel well.
 e Yes, I'd love to, thanks.
 f I fell off my bike and broke my arm.
 g Yes, we do. Here you are.
 h You choose. I don't mind.
 i No problem.

◯ / ⑧

Reading

9 Read the article and complete the sentences with one word.

Make the world a better place

Small actions can make the world better.

Start with your family

✤ Do some chores: hang out the washing or take out the rubbish. Your mum and dad will be happy.

✤ Give your parents a big hug and say you love them to make them feel good.

Do something nice for other people

✤ Invite new neighbours to your home. Make them feel welcome.

✤ Collect money and food for charity that helps poor people.

Do something for your neighbourhood too

✤ Clean up the streets with your friends so your neighbourhood can look nice.

✤ Plant trees and flowers in the park to make it more beautiful.

0 Small actions can make the world _better_.

1 Your parents will be _____ when you do some chores.

2 Tell your parents you love them and give them a big _____.

3 Make new _____ feel welcome – invite them to your home.

4 You can collect _____ and money to help poor people.

5 Your neighbourhood can look nice when you clean up the _____.

6 More flowers and _____ can make the park beautiful.

◯ / ⑥

© Pearson Education Limited 2019

PHOTOCOPIABLE

Listening	◯ / ⑥	Communication	◯ / ⑧
Reading	◯ / ⑥	**Your total score**	◯ / ⑳

name _____ class _____

Part 1 Reading and Writing

Read the email and write the missing words. Write one word on each line.

Hi Milly,

I'm sorry I can't meet you this afternoon. I'm busy today because I have a lot of chores.

Anna is lucky. She finished her chores an hour ⁰_ago_. She fed the animals, watered the plants and ¹_____ the table after breakfast. She is doing her homework right ²_____.

Max isn't as tidy ³_____ Anna and me. He's messy! He's in his room ⁴_____ the moment – I can hear him, but I don't think he is ⁵_____ his bed!

Dad is messy too. He lost the ⁶_____ control for the TV last night – again. I found it ⁷_____ I was vacuuming the living room. It was under the sofa! Mum is at work. She started her new job at the big department ⁸_____ in town last week.

⁹_____ you want to meet me in the park tomorrow afternoon?

Cheers,

Rosie

☐ / ⑨

© Pearson Education Limited 2019 | PHOTOCOPIABLE

name _____ class _____

© Pearson Education Limited 2019 | PHOTOCOPIABLE

Part 2 Reading and Writing

Look at the picture and read the story. Write some words to complete the sentences about the story. You can use 1, 2, 3 or 4 words.

Summer Holidays
by Tom Summers

Two years ago, my family and I went on holiday to London. My parents and I loved it, but my sister Julie didn't like it very much. She was only five. She got tired quickly and she didn't want to get up early in the mornings.

On the first day, we went sightseeing around the city on a red London bus. We saw a lot of famous places: the Tower of London, the Houses of Parliament and St Paul's Cathedral. In the evening, we went on a boat trip on the River Thames.

We did a lot of other things too. Mum loved London's famous department stores and spent a lot of money there. Dad spent his money in bookshops. I get bored in shops, so I didn't buy anything.

We visited some great museums. The Science Museum was fun, but the Natural History Museum was better. It had dinosaurs!

One day, we went to Hyde Park. We fed the ducks in the lake and we went cycling. Unfortunately, it was hot and my face and arms were red at the end of the day!

On our last day, my sister got lost. We were walking in Oxford Street when Mum said to Dad: 'Where's Julie? I thought she was with you!'

'And I thought she was with you!' said Dad.

Luckily, we found her quickly. She was looking at some toys in a shop window ten metres behind us!

Examples

0 Tom and *his parents* loved London.

0 *Julie* is Tom's sister.

Questions

1 Two years ago, Julie was _____ years old.

2 Tom and his family went around the city on a red _____.

3 They went on a _____ one evening.

4 Tom's mother went shopping in some famous _____.

5 Tom didn't buy things because he got _____ in shops.

6 Tom thought the Natural History Museum was _____ the Science Museum.

7 They went _____ in Hyde Park.

8 They lost Julie when _____ in Oxford Street.

9 When they found Julie, she was looking at toys _____.

☐ / ⑨

Exam Test

name _____ class _____

© Pearson Education Limited 2019 | PHOTOCOPIABLE

Part 3 Listening and Communication

🔊 **12** Listen and draw lines. There is one example.

Eddie   Alex   Clara   Joe

Sarah   Pete   Diana

☐ / ⑥

name   class

Steve wants to buy a birthday present for his sister. His friend Lily wants to help him. What are Lily's questions? Write them in the spaces. The first one is an example.

Example

Lily: *What's wrong, Steve?*

Questions

Steve: It's my sister's birthday next Saturday but I don't know what to buy her.

Lily: ¹ _____

Steve: Yes, please! I'd love your help.

Lily: ² _____

Steve: Yes, she does. She loves clothes.

Lily: ³ _____

Steve: Her favourite colour is red. She likes black too.

Lily: ⁴ _____

Steve: Small, I think.

Lily: ⁵ _____

Steve: No, I can't. I don't have a card.

Lily: ⁶ _____

Steve: I've got £20.

Lily: Great. The new clothes shop has got special offers this week. Let's go.

◻ / ⑥

Reading and Writing	◻ / ⑱
Listening and Communication	◻ / ⑫
Your total score	◻ / ㉚

© Pearson Education Limited 2019

PHOTOCOPIABLE

name _____   class _____

Part 1 Reading and Writing

Read the email and write the missing words. Write one word on each line.

Hi Philip,

Finally! We're here ⁰*in* the big city! Have you ¹_____ moved house?
It's very hard work! Dad ²_____ started his new job and he loves it.
Next week, I ³_____ starting at my new school. I'm a little nervous.

Our ⁴_____ of flats is on a busy street. We live on the sixth ⁵_____
and there's a great view from the balcony. When I wake ⁶_____
in the morning, I can see the park from my bedroom window. I think
I ⁷_____ be very happy here.

Today I must help Mum because she's not very well and she needs some
rest. She's lying on the sofa ⁸_____ now, so I'm making dinner tonight
– chips and a salad. I have to ⁹_____ some potatoes and fry them in
hot oil. I enjoy cooking.

See you at the weekend.

Jack

☐ / 9

© Pearson Education Limited 2019 PHOTOCOPIABLE

name _____ class _____

Part 2 Reading and Writing

Read the story. Choose a word from the box. Write the correct word next to numbers 1–8. There is one example.

| checked abroad muscles ambition broke neck runny enjoy going doctor ~~cold~~ |

When Natalie was a little girl, she loved outdoor activities. She played football and went cycling every day. Sometimes she had a ⁰_cold_ or a ¹_____ nose. She went to see the ²_____ when she had a temperature, but she never stayed in bed for a long time.

When Natalie was seventeen, she fell off her horse and ³_____ a leg and an arm. She spent weeks in hospital. But she exercised every day and her bones and ⁴_____ quickly became stronger. Six months later, she was strong enough to go hiking and rock climbing.

Now Natalie is twenty-four and she lives ⁵_____. Two years ago, she got a job in Spain. 'I love living here and I am happy and healthy,' she says. 'The first time I came to this place, I ⁶_____ out the outdoor activities you can do. There are so many!'

Natalie's ⁷_____ is to have her own business in Spain one day. In the future, she wants to have an adventure camp. I'm sure people will ⁸_____ going there!

Now choose the best name for this story. Tick (✓) one box.

A dangerous sport ☐
Winter sports ☐
A sporty girl ☐

☐ / ⑨

© Pearson Education Limited 2019   PHOTOCOPIABLE

name   class

Part 3 Listening and Communication

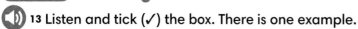 13 Listen and tick (✓) the box. There is one example.

Example:

0 What has Steve done?

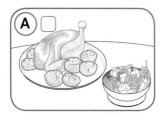 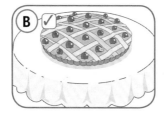 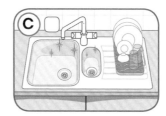

Questions:

1 How is Steve cooking the potatoes?

2 What does Steve want to be when he leaves school?

3 What does Steve have to wash now?

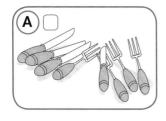  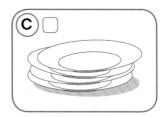

4 Where is Steve's sister?

5 What time is Steve's father coming home?

© Pearson Education Limited 2019 | PHOTOCOPIABLE

/ 5

name   class

Part 4 Listening and Communication

It's Friday afternoon. Kathy and Rose are talking about their weekend plans. What does Rose say? Read the conversation and choose the best answer. Write a letter (A–J) for each answer. You do not need to use all the letters. There is one example.

Example

0 Kathy: I'm going to the new shopping centre this afternoon. Can you come?

Rose: *E*

Questions

1 Kathy: What's wrong with her?

Rose: _____

2 Kathy: Is it a bad injury?

Rose: _____

3 Kathy: Poor cat! Do you want to hang out tomorrow?

Rose: _____

4 Kathy: How about Sunday? Are you free?

Rose: _____

5 Kathy: Great. Would you like to go to the beach or to the skate park?

Rose: _____

6 Kathy: Do you like windsurfing?

Rose: _____

7 Kathy: I'm sure you'll love it. Let's do that! What time should we meet?

Rose: _____

A I agree with you.

B After ten o'clock. You know I hate getting up early at the weekend.

C Yes, she can't walk.

D I don't know. I've never tried it.

E I'm sorry, I can't come. I'm taking the cat to the vet.

F She put a plaster on it.

G Yes, I am.

H You choose. I don't mind.

I She's got a cut on her foot.

J I'd love to, but we're visiting my grandparents tomorrow.

◻ / ⑦

© Pearson Education Limited 2019   PHOTOCOPIABLE

Reading and Writing	◻ / ⑱
Listening and Communication	◻ / ⑫
Your total score	◻ / ㉚

© Pearson Education Limited 2019 | PHOTOCOPIABLE

1&2 Speaking Tasks

Notes for the teacher

- **Vocabulary:** household chores, personality adjectives, shopping, shops
- **Grammar:** utterances using the Present Simple, the Present Continuous, stative verbs, comparative and superlative adjectives, *too, not … enough, (not) as … as*

Task 1: Ask the student to look at the picture. Then ask the questions.

- It's Saturday morning and the Smith family are at home. What are they doing?
- What other household chores do you think they do at the weekend?
- Compare the people in the family. [To elicit: *younger/older than, the youngest/oldest*]
- Compare the family pets. [To elicit: *bigger/smaller than, the biggest/smallest, not as big as*]
- Compare the kitchen and the living room. [To elicit: *cleaner/ tidier/dirtier than, (not) as clean/tidy/dirty as*]

Task 2: Ask the student to talk about himself/ herself. Use these questions to help.

- What household chores do you do?
- What household chores do the other members of your family do?
- Who is the tidiest person in your family? Who is the messiest?
- Where do your parents go to buy bread?
- Where do your parents go to buy fruit and vegetables?
- How do your parents pay for things?
- Do you like shopping? Why / Why not?
- What are your favourite shops?

© Pearson Education Limited 2019 PHOTOCOPIABLE

&4 Speaking Tasks

Notes for the teacher

- **Vocabulary:** going on holiday, useful things, smartphones
- **Grammar:** utterances using the Past Simple, the Past Continuous, adverbs of manner

Task 1: Ask the student to look at the picture. Then ask the questions.

- This is a photo of the Brown family on their holiday last year. What country did they go to?
- What did Mrs Brown take with her?
- Where do you think they went that day and what did they do there? [To elicit: *the beach, swimming, snorkelling*]
- What were they doing that afternoon at 5 o'clock?
- Was Charlie walking fast?
- Was the musician playing well?
- What electrical items can you see in the picture?

Task 2: Ask the student to talk about himself/herself. Use these questions to help.

- What did you do on your last holiday?
- Where did you go and where did you stay?
- Who did you go with?
- Describe a funny, interesting or silly thing that happened to you on holiday.
- What useful things did you take with you?
- What electrical items do you use at home every day and every week?

© Pearson Education Limited 2019 | PHOTOCOPIABLE

5&6 Speaking Tasks

Notes for the teacher

- **Vocabulary:** health problems, injuries, cooking (verbs and nouns), serving, eating and describing food
- **Grammar:** utterances using *have to*, *should*, the Present Perfect

Task 1: Ask the student to look at the picture. Then ask the questions.

- The White family are at home. What's wrong with Mr White?
- What should he do?
- What's happened to Mrs White?
- What shouldn't she do?
- What has Oscar done?
- What has Hannah made?
- What should Oscar do?

Task 2: Ask the student to talk about himself/ herself. Use these questions to help.

- Have you ever broken an arm or a leg?
- Have you ever had a stomachache?
- What can you do when you have a headache?
- What should you do when have the flu?
- Have you ever made soup or any other food?
- Do you know how to make a simple dish (e.g. a salad, chips, a simple cake, soup)?
- What ingredients and other things do you need to make it? What do you need to do?

© Pearson Education Limited 2019

PHOTOCOPIABLE

&8 Speaking Tasks

Notes for the teacher

- **Vocabulary:** places to live, parts of the house, life ambitions, being with people, good manners
- **Grammar:** utterances using *must*, *mustn't*, *can* and *will* for predictions

Task 1: Ask the student to look at the picture. Then ask the questions.

- Where is this street? [To elicit: *in a city*]
- What kind of houses can you see? Describe them.
- What are the people in the street doing?
- What should people do when they take their dog for a walk?
- What should people do when they meet a neighbour?

Task 2: Ask the student to talk about himself/ herself. Use these questions to help.

- Where do you live?
- What kind of home do you have? Describe it.
- Where do you think you will live in the future?
- What do you think you will do in the future? What are your ambitions?
- Are your friends/classmates/neighbours polite?
- Think about the rules in your house / at your school. What can/must/mustn't you do?

Unit 1 Life at home

Write 70-80 words about the things you do every weekend. Use questions 1-5 to help you.

1 What do you usually do when you get up on Saturday morning?
2 What chores do you do at the weekend?
3 What chores do your family do?
4 What do you do with your friends at the weekend?
5 What do you like doing with your family at the weekend?

Unit 2 Shopping

Your cousin wants to buy your sister headphones for her birthday. Write an email to your cousin. Give your opinion of the headphones in the table and say which ones are better. Give three arguments.

	AudioX headphones	Sound01 headphones
Price	£39.99	£79.99
Size, weight	small, light (easy to take them with you)	big, heavy
Colour	silver, gold, black, red	black
Sound	good	very good

Unit 3 Going on holiday

You were on holiday a few weeks ago. Write an email (70-80 words) to your friend and tell him/her about it. Use questions 1-4 to help you.

1 Where did you go on holiday?
2 Who did you go with?
3 What did you do?
4 What didn't you do?

Unit 4 Useful things

Write 70-80 words about something interesting that happened to you. Use questions 1-6 to help you.

1 When and where did it happen?
2 What were you doing before it happened?
3 What were the other people doing?
4 What was the main event?
5 What happened next?
6 How did you feel?

Unit 5 Health matters

Write 70-80 words giving advice about how to keep healthy. Use questions 1-6 to help you.

1 How important is good health?
2 What should you eat and drink?
3 What shouldn't you eat and drink?
4 Why do you have to exercise?
5 What kind of exercise can you do?
6 How much should you sleep?

Unit 6 Cooking and eating

Look at the pictures and write a recipe for an apple cake. Use questions 1-3 to help you.

1 What ingredients do you need? Write a list.
2 What other things, e.g. a knife, a bowl do you need?
3 How do you make it? Write the instructions.

Unit 7 Where I live

You are meeting some friends this weekend. Write an email (70-80 words) to your cousin and invite him/her to join you. Use questions 1-5 to help you.

1 Invite your cousin to spend the weekend with you.
2 Who are you meeting?
3 Where are you meeting?
4 What are you doing on Saturday?
5 What are you doing on Sunday?

Unit 8 A happy life

Write 70-80 words making predictions about your life in the future. Use questions 1-4 to help you.

1 What job will you have?
2 Will you have a family / a lot of friends?
3 Where will you live?
4 What are your other ambitions?

© Pearson Education Limited 2019 | PHOTOCOPIABLE

Audio script

🔊 2 Skills Test 1&2
Exercise 1

S: Stella   M: Mum

S: Mum, what can we buy Grandad for his birthday?
M: Well, Stella, he needs a new jacket – something stylish.
S: And I think he also needs a shirt.
M: Good idea. Oh look! There's a lovely jacket in that shop window!
S: Where?
M: There. In the department store.
S: Yes, it *is* nice. But it's so expensive! £150!
M: Yes, that's too much. Let's look at the clothes in the clothes shop next to the chemist's.
S: All right. … Oh! I like this dark blue shirt, and it's only £19.
M: And look at this grey jacket.
S: It's very stylish. And the price isn't too high.
M: Well, Stella, you can buy the shirt and I can buy the jacket.
S: What size is Grandad?
M: Medium. Now, let me see how much money I have. Hmm … I can't pay in cash, but I can pay by card.
S: And I can pay in cash.
M: OK. Then we can go to the café next to the bookshop. It's time for lunch.
S: Great.

🔊 3 Skills Test 1&2
Exercise 2

U: Uncle   E: Eddie

U: So, who do you hang out with, Eddie?
E: Colin. He's my best friend and we do everything together.
U: Are you the same age?
E: Yes, we are. We are both thirteen.
U: What is Colin like? Is he like you?
E: No! We're different. I'm not bossy, but Colin *loves* telling people what to do. A lot of people don't like this, but I don't mind. I'm easy-going and I never get angry.
U: That's interesting.
E: Colin is a little loud and he talks a lot, but I don't – and I'm a good listener.
U: Are you in the same class at school?
E: Yes, we are. It's funny, we're both intelligent, but Colin is bad at Maths and I'm bad at English, so I help him and he helps me. We do our homework at my home because Colin's bedroom is untidy. I can't work in an untidy room. I like things to be in the right place.
U: What other things do you do together?
E: We play chess and football. I'm sporty, but Colin's the best player in the school. He wants to be a footballer.
U: What about you?
E: Me? I want to be a scientist.

🔊 4 Skills Test 3&4
Exercise 1

O: Oliver   C: Cathy

O: Hi, Cathy! When did you get back from your holiday?
C: Last Sunday.
O: Where did you go?
C: To Valencia.
O: That's in Spain, isn't it?
C: Yes, it is. My grandma lives there, she's Spanish. We had a fantastic time.
O: Where did you stay? At your grandma's house?
C: No, we stayed in a hotel in the centre of the city. There were lots of restaurants there, and we tried the local food. We loved it!
O: What else did you do?
C: Lots of things. On our first day, we visited Grandma. On the second day, we explored the city. It's very old, but it's got some fantastic modern buildings. On the third day, we visited a museum. Oh! And we saw Anna Smart!
O: Anna Smart, the actor?
C: Yes!
O: Where did you see her?
C: In a café. Mum and I were having orange juice, when Anna came in. I asked for a selfie and she said yes!
O: Your brother really likes her, doesn't he?
C: Yes! Poor Jack. He wasn't with Mum and me. He was on a boat trip with Dad. So, I've got a photo of me with Anna Smart, and Jack has a photo of him on a boat!

🔊 5 Skills Test 3&4
Exercise 2

N: Narrator   B: Boy   G: Girl   W: Woman
M: Man

N: **Example**
B: I do my school projects on my computer. I save the projects on the computer and on this thing. That way I never lose my work.
N: **One**
G: I always wash my hair after I go swimming, because swimming pool water is very bad for it. I use this when I want to dry my hair quickly.
N: **Two**
B: It is connected to the TV in the living room. We often use it to watch a film in the evening. We've got a great collection of films on DVD.
N: **Three**
G: Mum bought it last week. It wasn't expensive – it was on special offer. Charlie uses it to make smoothies with yoghurt, strawberries and honey. Very healthy.
N: **Four**
W: I love it. It's a bit noisy, but when I use it, I can feel that my teeth are really clean. I charge it two or three times a week.
N: **Five**
M: I like reading about different countries before I visit them. I bought this one before we went to Poland. It tells you about the most interesting places, the best restaurants, the best shops.

🔊 6 Skills Test 5&6
Exercise 1

N: Narrator   M: Mum   E: Emily

N: **Example. What time is it?**
M: Emily, I need your help. It's half past four and we have to get ready for the dinner party tonight. It starts at eight o'clock. Your dad comes home at quarter to seven, so it's too late for him to help.
E: Of course, Mum.

N: **One. What does Emily's mum have to do first?**
M: There's so much to do!
E: Do you want me to make the salad?
M: No, I can make the salad later. I have to make the cake first. Then, I can roast the meat and potatoes. Can you wash the strawberries for the cake, please?
N: **Two. What should Emily do last?**
E: Should I set the table?
M: Yes, but first vacuum the carpet and put the flowers in the living room. Then set the table. Use the best knives and forks.
N: **Three. What has Emily's mum broken?**
E: What happened, Mum?
M: I was putting some mugs, cups and glasses in the dishwasher and I dropped a mug. Can you help me clean up the mess on the floor, dear?
E: OK, Mum.
N: **Four. What ingredients does Emily have to buy?**
M: Oh no!
E: What's wrong?
M: I haven't got all the ingredients … Potatoes, yes … tomatoes, yes … but no onions. Please run to the greengrocer's and buy some.
E: How many should I buy?
M: Two, please.
N: **Five. What has Emily's mum got on her hand?**
E: OK, Mum. I've chopped the onions.
M: Did you get that cut when you were chopping them?
E: Yes, I did. … But what's that on *your* hand? A burn?
M: No, it's a mosquito bite from last night! … OK, let's get ready for our guests.

🔊 7 Skills Test 5&6
Exercise 2

M: Man

M: And now my recipe for French toast. It's delicious, it's easy and it's my family's favourite breakfast. The ingredients are simple. Most people have them in their kitchen. You need three eggs. You also need one and a half cups of milk, a little salt, some sugar and butter … um … what else? … Yes! Bread! You can't make French toast without bread!
Now, beat the ingredients together very well in a large bowl. Not the bread, of course – only the eggs and milk! Add a little salt. Then, slice the bread – you need eight pieces of bread for this recipe. Next, put the bread in the egg and milk mixture. Then put a little butter in a frying pan. When it's hot, fry the bread for two minutes on each side. Finally, put a little sugar on the bread and fry it again for about 15 seconds on each side. Serve the French toast with jam, honey or fruit. Lovely!

🔊 8 Skills Test 7&8
Exercise 1

B: Billy   S: Sue

B: Where *are* they? Where?! Oh! Where?!
S: What's the matter, Billy?
B: I *must* find them!
S: Find what? What are you looking for?
B: A USB stick and a portable charger.
S: Here they are.

B: Oh wow! You've found them! Where were they?

S: Well, the USB stick was in this drawer and the charger was on the bookcase.

B: But those are *my* things. I'm not looking for *those*.

S: Whose things *are* you looking for, then?

B: *Mum's* USB stick and *Dad's* portable charger. Mum said I could borrow them, but I mustn't lose them. I thought they were on my desk, but they weren't there when I woke up this morning.

S: Oooh! Mum will be angry when she finds out! When was the last time you used them?

B: Hmm … last night. I charged my mobile phone, and I used the USB stick when I was doing my homework.

S: What did you do after you finished your homework?

B: I went outside on the balcony for a few minutes. Then I went to the kitchen for a glass of water.

S: Have you looked there? Maybe you left them on the balcony or near the kitchen sink. Don't worry. I'm sure you'll find them.

B: I hope you're right.

🔊 9 Skills Test 7&8
Exercise 2

B: Becky

B: Hello, I'm Becky. I'm fourteen and I live in a big city. Two months ago, the people in my block of flats decided to do something together to make our neighbourhood a better place.
All the flats in our building have balconies, but some of them didn't look very nice. First, we decided to clean up our balconies. Then, we put some flowers in flower pots on each balcony. Some people even planted small trees in big flower pots or old bins, but our balcony isn't big enough for a tree. Mum and I put a bird bath with clean water on our balcony. I hope birds will come to drink the water or wash.
Next, we bought some second-hand chairs for the balconies. They were cheap, and we painted them red, blue, green or yellow. We now have the prettiest balconies in the city! When the weather is good, we can sit outside and talk – our balconies are very close together! Next month, we're having a balcony party with cakes, sandwiches and music. We hope our neighbourhood will be a friendlier place in the future. And it will be greener too!

🔊 10 Mid-Year Test 1–4
Exercise 7

A: Adam L: Linda

A: Linda! Put away your clothes before you go. And make your bed!

L: Stop telling me what to do, Adam! You're so bossy!

A: And you're the messiest person I know!

L: No, I'm not.

A: Yes, you are. You didn't make your bed yesterday or the day before. And you lose your things all the time.

L: No, I don't.

A: Yes, you do. When you went to Italy with your class, you lost your hairdryer … no, I'm wrong, it wasn't your hairdryer, it was your electric toothbrush. How can you lose a *toothbrush*?

L: I didn't lose it! I left it at the hotel. Now I need to buy a new one.

A: Are you going to the department store?

L: Yes, I am.

A: Can you buy me a USB stick?

L: How much are USB sticks?

A: They aren't expensive. They're on special offer this week. They were £6.99, but now they're £4.99.

L: Oh, I don't have enough money to pay in cash and I can't pay by card because, well, I can't find it.

A: I can give you some money … and don't forget to get a receipt. Oh! And please buy a newspaper for Mum.

L: At the newsagent's?

A: Yes, you know, the one next to the sports shop.

L: Oh, all right.

A: Thanks.

🔊 11 End-of-Year Test 1–8
Exercise 7

N: Narrator B: Ben M: Molly D: Duncan
O: Olivia S: Stuart

N: Ben

B: I often have earache after I go snorkelling. Sometimes the earache goes away quickly, but sometimes I have to see the doctor. She says the problem is some water stays in my ear. But I can't stop snorkelling! I love it.

N: Molly

M: I got headaches when I read a lot or looked at a computer screen for a long time and my eyes got tired. My headaches stopped when I went to the eye doctor and started wearing glasses.

N: Duncan

D: I had the flu six months ago. I had a temperature, I coughed and I had a sore throat. I was ill for eight days. I asked the doctor what to do and she said: 'Stay in bed, drink a lot of warm tea and rest.'

N: Olivia

O: We went camping last week and I had a lot of mosquito bites because I didn't use a mosquito net. Mum put lemon juice on the bites and they felt better. Dad says cold tea is also good. I'll try it next time.

N: Stuart

S: Some people can eat everything, but I can't. When I eat too much, I have a stomachache. Spicy food also gives me a stomachache sometimes. I feel better when I drink mint tea. Granny says bananas, rice or toast are also good for a stomachache.

🔊 12 Exam Test 1–4
Part 3

N: Narrator L: Lucy U: Uncle Dave

N: Listen and look. There is one example.

L: Hi, Uncle Dave.

U: Hi, Lucy! Are these your friends?

L: Yes, they are. Can you see the girl with the jeans and T-shirt? She's looking at postcards.

U: Yes.

L: That's Diana, my best friend.

N: Can you see the line? This is an example. Now you listen and draw lines.

U: Who's that boy?

L: Which one?

U: The short boy. He's checking the price of that model boat.

L: Oh, that's Pete. He's Diana's brother.

U: Who is the tall boy standing in the queue?

L: I don't know. But the girl with the shopping basket is Sarah. She's very funny! … Can you see that boy over there? He's paying the cashier. That's Eddie. He's buying a teddy for his little brother.

U: Do you know the girl near the door?

L: Yes, that's Clara. She's bored. She hates shopping. … My friend Joe doesn't like shopping either.

U: Which one is Joe?

L: Can you see the boy with the mobile phone?

U: Yes, I see him.

L: And the boy over there, with the dark hair, is Alex.

U: The boy reading the guidebook?

L: That's right. He's the most intelligent student in the class.

U: You've got a lot of friends, Lucy.

L: Yes, I have.

N: Now listen to Part three again.

🔊 13 Exam Test 5–8
Part 3

N: Narrator S: Steve A: Aunt May

N: Listen and look. There is one example. What has Steve done?

S: Hello, Aunt May! How are you?

A: Hello, Steve. I'm fine, thank you. What are you doing this afternoon?

S: I've baked a cake.

A: That's nice.

S: And I also want to make dinner and clean the kitchen.

N: Can you see the tick? Now you listen and tick the box.

N: One. How is Steve cooking the potatoes?

A: What are you making for dinner?

S: Chicken and potatoes.

A: Are you roasting the potatoes?

S: No, and I don't want to fry them. I'm boiling them. I'm going to serve them with butter.

N: Two. What does Steve want to be when he leaves school?

A: You're a good cook, Steve. Would you like to work in a restaurant one day?

S: That's not a bad idea! Dad says I should be a teacher because I'm patient, but I want to be a dentist.

A: Really? That's interesting!

N: Three. What does Steve have to wash now?

A: Have you set the table?

S: No, I haven't. I've washed the best plates, knives and forks. Now I have to wash the glasses. I will put some flowers from the garden on the table too.

N: Four. Where is Steve's sister?

A: Is your sister helping you?

S: Emma? No. She's upstairs.

A: Oh! Is she doing her homework?

S: No, she isn't in her bedroom. She was cleaning the attic and she got dirty, so she's having a shower.

N: Five. What time is Steve's father coming home?

A: When are your mum and dad coming home today?

S: Dad is usually home at half past five, but today he's coming home late – at half past six. Mum is coming home early today – at five o'clock.

A: Well, tell your mum and dad I called. And have a lovely dinner.

N: Now listen to Part three again.

Answer key

Placement Test

Exercise 1
A: 1 rubber 2 jar 3 meat
4 tablet 5 island 6 forest
B: 1 hospital 2 carton
3 keyboard 4 cereal
5 laptop 6 bank

Exercise 2
A: 1 chat 2 make 3 do
4 Get 5 visit 6 look
B: 1 do 2 stay 3 walk 4 Get
5 text 6 tidy

Exercise 3
A: 1 a 2 b 3 c 4 a 5 c 6 a
B: 1 c 2 b 3 b 4 a 5 c 6 b

Exercise 4
A: 1 card 2 greengrocer's
3 Peel 4 blender 5 burn
6 balcony 7 sink
B: 1 greengrocer's
2 cupboard 3 balcony
4 Peel 5 cut 6 card
7 blender

Exercise 5
A: 1 is watching 2 studies
3 know 4 don't visit 5 are
they making 6 Does Amy
play 7 am not working
B: 1 don't get 2 is having
3 want 4 Does Max play
5 are you watching 6 am
not helping 7 studies

Exercise 6
A: 1 quietly 2 much 3 any
4 too 5 the longest 6 as
organised 7 Whose
B: 1 Whose 2 any 3 much
4 as patient 5 quietly 6 too
7 the hottest

Exercise 7
A: 1 wasn't 2 didn't study
3 went 4 were 5 Did you
make 6 met 7 Were you
B: 1 went 2 Did you eat
3 wasn't 4 were 5 made
6 Were you 7 didn't study

Exercise 8
A: 1 were you 2 stayed 3 has
4 never 5 shouldn't 6 must
7 mustn't
B: 1 were you 2 tried 3 never
4 has 5 mustn't 6 must
7 shouldn't

Exercise 9
A: 1 are 2 will 3 to 4 doesn't
5 won't 6 going 7 has
B: 1 has 2 are 3 won't
4 doesn't 5 to 6 will
7 going

Exercise 10
A: 1 would you like
2 a moment 3 In my
opinion 4 Can I borrow
5 Here you are
B: 1 In my opinion
2 Here you are
3 Would you like
4 Is it OK 5 I'm afraid

Exercise 11
A: 1 c 2 b 3 f 4 a 5 e
B: 1 d 2 b 3 c 4 f 4 a

Vocabulary Check 1

Exercise 1
A: 1 load 2 put 3 iron
4 empty 5 vacuum 6 set
7 water
B: 1 vacuum 2 iron 3 load
4 set 5 put 6 water
7 empty

Exercise 2
A: 1 c 2 e 3 a 4 d 5 b
B: 1 e 2 b 3 c 4 d 5 a

Exercise 3
A: 1 loud 2 quiet
3 easy-going 4 bossy
5 messy 6 organised 7 tidy
8 patient
B: 1 bossy 2 organised
3 patient 4 quiet 5 loud
6 tidy 7 messy
8 easy-going

Vocabulary Check 2

Exercise 1
A: 1 shopping trolley
2 shopping bag 3 special
offer 4 shopping basket
5 cashier 6 shopping list
B: 1 special offer 2 cashier
3 shopping trolley
4 shopping list 5 shopping
bag 6 shopping basket

Exercise 2
A: 1 shopping 2 card 3 cash
4 change 5 receipt 6 carry
B: 1 stand 2 shopping 3 cash
4 card 5 receipt 6 carry

Exercise 3
A: 1 sports shop 2 chemist's
3 shoe shop 4 bookshop
5 baker's 6 newsagent's
7 greengrocer's 8 clothes
shop
B: 1 newsagent's 2 chemist's
3 baker's 4 clothes shop
5 greengrocer's 6 sports
shop 7 bookshop 8 shoe
shop

Vocabulary Check 3

Exercise 1
A: 1 cycling 2 guided
tour 3 hiking 4 beach
5 camping 6 boat trip
7 snorkelling 8 try, food
9 explore 10 day trip
B: 1 boat trip 2 beach
3 explore 4 cycling
5 camping 6 guided tour
7 day trip 8 snorkelling
9 hiking 10 try, food

Exercise 2
A: 1 dark 2 cold 3 tired
4 lost 5 bored
B: 1 tired 2 dark 3 lost
4 cold 5 bored

Vocabulary Check 4

Exercise 1
A: 1 smart TV 2 DVD player
3 USB stick 4 hairdryer
5 electric toothbrush
6 remote control 7 games
console 8 blender
9 toaster 10 microwave
oven
B: 1 USB stick 2 DVD player
3 toaster 4 games
console 5 smart TV
6 electric toothbrush
7 hairdryer 8 microwave
oven 9 blender 10 remote
control

Exercise 2
A: 1 off 2 Unplug 3 in 4 on
B: 1 Unplug 2 on 3 off 4 in

Exercise 3
A: 1 battery 2 ringtone 3 app
4 Wi-Fi 5 touch screen
6 portable charger
B: 1 Wi-Fi 2 portable charger
3 ringtone 4 touch screen
5 battery 6 app

Vocabulary Check 5

Exercise 1
A: 1 cold, runny, sneezes
2 coughs 3 stomachache
4 headache, temperature
5 blocked 6 toothache
7 sore throat
B: 1 sore throat 2 toothache
3 blocked 4 headache,
temperature
5 stomachache 6 coughs
7 cold, runny, sneezes

Exercise 2
A: 1 bruise 2 bites 3 broken
4 cut 5 burn
B: 1 burn 2 bites 3 cut
4 broken 5 bruise

Exercise 3
A: 1 b 2 d 3 a 4 e 5 c
B: 1 a 2 c 3 e 4 b 5 d

Vocabulary Check 6

Exercise 1
A: 1 oven 2 Chop 3 pan
4 Peel 5 pot 6 Boil 7 Slice
8 bowl 9 Bake 10 tin
B: 1 oven 2 Bake 3 tin
4 Slice 5 bowl 6 Chop
7 pan 8 Peel 9 pot
10 Boil

Exercise 2
A: 1 spoon 2 knife 3 fork
4 glass 5 cup
B: 1 fork 2 cup 3 knife
4 spoon 5 glass

Exercise 3
A: 1 delicious 2 sour 3 salty
4 disgusting 5 spicy
B: 1 disgusting 2 spicy 3 sour
4 salty 5 delicious

Vocabulary Check 7

Exercise 1
A: 1 flat 2 block 3 balcony
4 lift 5 cottage 6 village
7 attic 8 semi-detached
9 stairs
B: 1 block 2 lift 3 floor
4 balcony 5 semi-detached
6 stairs 7 attic 8 cottage
9 village

Exercise 2
A: 1 tap 2 mirror 3 sink
4 drawer 5 cupboard
6 bookcase
B: 1 bookcase 2 cupboard
3 sink 4 tap 5 mirror
6 drawer

Exercise 3
A: 1 out 2 out 3 up 4 for
5 up
B: 1 up 2 up 3 out 4 for
5 out

Vocabulary Check 8

Exercise 1
A: 1 be 2 learn 3 live 4 have
5 be 6 have 7 learn 8 be
9 have 10 live
B: 1 be 2 live 3 learn 4 have
5 learn 6 be 7 have
8 have 9 be 10 live

Exercise 2
A: 1 give 2 invite 3 visit
4 shake 5 kiss
B: 1 shake 2 give 3 visit
4 invite 5 kiss

Exercise 3
A: 1 on 2 late 3 permission
4 turn 5 interrupt
B: 1 late 2 on 3 turn
4 interrupt 5 permission

Grammar Check 1

Exercise 1
A: 1 isn't doing 2 'm
vacuuming 3 is ironing
4 are making 5 Is he
loading
B: 1 isn't doing 2 is cooking
3 'm watering 4 are
hanging 5 Is he taking

Exercise 2
A: 1 wants 2 don't
understand 3 Do you know
4 'm making, need
B: 1 need 2 wants
3 'm doing, don't
understand 4 Do you know

Exercise 3
A: 1 is wearing 2 don't go
3 Is Gran sleeping 4 tidy
5 is taking
B: 1 Is Mum working 2 'm
loading 3 tidies 4 is
wearing 5 don't go

Answer key

Grammar Check 2

Exercise 1
A: 1 the fastest 2 the biggest 3 better 4 the most expensive 5 more organised 6 sportier 7 worse

B: 1 the sportiest 2 bigger 3 the best 4 faster 5 worse 6 more expensive 7 the most organised

Exercise 2
A: 1 too expensive 2 clean enough 3 too young 4 interesting enough

B: 1 too dirty 2 cheap enough 3 too boring 4 old enough

Exercise 3
A: 1 is as (short) as 2 is as (intelligent) as 3 isn't as (messy) as 4 isn't as (strong) as

B: 1 is as (intelligent) as 2 isn't as (tidy) as 3 is as (tall) as 4 isn't as (fast) as

Grammar Check 3

Exercise 1
A: 1 didn't go 2 took 3 visited 4 swam 5 didn't have 6 went 7 was

B: 1 went 2 didn't take 3 swam 4 visited 5 didn't stay 6 had 7 was

Exercise 2
A: 1 Was the weather; it was 2 Did Emily take; she didn't 3 Were Jake and Kim; they weren't 4 Did you and Sam go; we did

B: 1 Were you and Jim; we weren't 2 Did Liz and Kevin explore; they did 3 Did Fred forget; he didn't 4 Was the weather; it was

Grammar Check 4

Exercise 1
A: 1 was playing 2 weren't watching 3 were you doing 4 wasn't surfing 5 Was (Jim) looking

B: 1 were they doing 2 wasn't watching 3 was studying 4 Was (Anna) using 5 weren't playing

Exercise 2
A: 1 were using, fell 2 were shopping, saw 3 Was she having, arrived

B: 1 Was he surfing, started 2 were having, arrived 3 were buying, saw

Exercise 3
A: 1 happily 2 quietly 3 well 4 loudly

B: 1 well 2 easily 3 quietly 4 loudly

Grammar Check 5

Exercise 1
A: 1 don't have to work 2 has to practise 3 doesn't have to stay 4 have to help 5 don't have to go

B: 1 has to help 2 don't have to do 3 have to practise 4 don't have to work 5 doesn't have to stay

Exercise 2
A: 1 do (we) have to 2 Does (Jack) have to 3 does (she) have to 4 Do (they) have to

B: 1 Do (we) have to 2 does (he) have to 3 Does (Maria) have to 4 do (they) have to

Exercise 3
A: 1 should 2 should I 3 should 4 Should I 5 shouldn't

B: 1 should 2 shouldn't 3 Should I 4 should 5 should I

Grammar Check 6

Exercise 1
A: 1 has left 2 haven't chopped, have washed 3 hasn't eaten 4 have had 5 have made 6 hasn't tidied

B: 1 has eaten 2 have made 3 have left 4 haven't tidied 5 hasn't had 6 have washed, haven't sliced

Exercise 2
A: 1 Has Ted ever tried 2 he has never tried 3 Have they won 4 have 5 Has your sister ever made 6 she has never made 7 Have you ever had 8 haven't

B: 1 Have you had 2 haven't 3 Has Tess ever heard 4 she has never heard 5 Have they ever worked 6 they have never worked 7 Has she ever won 8 has

Grammar Check 7

Exercise 1
A: 1 are studying 2 Are you coming 3 is picking 4 'm going 5 are your parents flying 6 aren't staying 7 'm not going

B: 1 are playing 2 Are you coming 3 'm going 4 is picking 5 are your cousins arriving 6 aren't taking 7 'm not doing

Exercise 2
A: 1 mustn't 2 can 3 can 4 mustn't 5 must 6 can 7 mustn't 8 must

B: 1 can 2 mustn't 3 must 4 mustn't 5 can 6 mustn't 7 can 8 must

Grammar Check 8

Exercise 1
A: 1 'll pass 2 won't be, 'll be 3 Will you go 4 will have 5 Will she enjoy 6 will they buy 7 won't live

B: 1 won't have 2 will they buy 3 'll pass 4 Will you enjoy 5 won't live 6 won't be, 'll be 7 Will she go

Exercise 2
A: 1 What 2 will 3 Why 4 does 5 did 6 were 7 is

B: 1 Why 2 did 3 is 4 were 5 does 6 will 7 What

Language Test
Get started!

Exercise 1
A: 1 hospital 2 tram 3 chef 4 restaurant 5 bike

B: 1 restaurant 2 bike 3 doctor 4 hospital 5 tram

Exercise 2
A: 1 canteen 2 staff room 3 History 4 in 5 about

B: 1 library 2 staff room 3 Maths 4 in 5 about

Exercise 3
A: 1 c 2 a 3 c 4 b 5 c

B: 1 b 2 c 3 a 4 b 5 c

Exercise 4
A: 1 don't have 2 often hang out 3 Do you go 4 usually meet 5 does Jess live 6 lives

B: 1 don't have 2 usually hang out 3 Does Martin live 4 lives 5 always walk 6 do you go

Exercise 5
A: 1 Are, going to study 2 'm going to watch 3 aren't going to get up 4 Is, going to walk

B: 1 'm going to see 2 aren't going to watch 3 Are, going to study 4 Is, going to get up

Exercise 6
A: 1 Is there 2 any 3 isn't 4 some 5 There aren't

B: 1 isn't 2 Is there 3 There aren't 4 some 5 any

Language Test 1

Exercise 1
A: 1 plants 2 table 3 dishwasher 4 living room 5 washing 6 bed

B: 1 table 2 rooms 3 washing machine 4 bed 5 washing 6 plants

Exercise 2
A: 1 d 2 c 3 e 4 b 5 a 6 f

B: 1 c 2 f 3 a 4 d 5 e 6 b

Exercise 3
A: 1 They aren't making their beds. 2 Is she setting the table for dinner? 3 I'm tidying my bedroom right now. 4 What are you cooking?

B: 1 I'm playing a game right now. 2 They aren't setting the table. 3 Is he making lunch for the family? 4 What are you watching?

Exercise 4
A: 1 is doing, knows 2 love, are playing

B: 1 are doing, know 2 is playing, loves

Exercise 5
A: 1 are making 2 watches 3 is playing 4 doesn't play 5 isn't winning

B: 1 are making 2 does 3 isn't studying 4 is watching 5 doesn't do

Exercise 6
A: 1 of course 2 I'm sorry 3 Can I help you 4 thank you 5 Do you need

B: 1 No problem 2 Can I help you 3 Do you need 4 that's fine 5 I'm sorry

Language Test 2

Exercise 1
A: 1 trolley 2 offer 3 check 4 queue 5 card 6 cash 7 change

B: 1 basket 2 price 3 special 4 stand 5 cash 6 card 7 receipt

Exercise 2
A: 1 shoe shop 2 greengrocer's 3 newsagent's 4 baker's 5 clothes shop

B: 1 newsagent's 2 clothes shop 3 shoe shop 4 greengrocer's 5 baker's

Exercise 3
A: 1 This shop is bigger than that shop. 2 Books are more expensive than magazines. 3 These jeans are more stylish than those trousers. 4 My coat is warmer than your jacket.

B: 1 Your jacket is warmer than my hoodie. 2 That shop is bigger than this shop. 3 Oranges are more expensive than apples. 4 Those boots are more stylish than these shoes.

Exercise 4
A: 1 longer 2 the funniest 3 more organised 4 the best

B: 1 the best 2 the messiest 3 more patient 4 shorter

Exercise 5
A: 1 too 2 as 3 enough 4 as 5 too

B: 1 too 2 as 3 too 4 enough 5 as

Exercise 6
A: 1 d 2 f 3 c 4 a 5 e

B: 1 d 2 c 3 e 4 f 5 a

Answer key

Language Test 3

Exercise 1
A: 1 explore 2 trips 3 guided
4 try 5 camping 6 hiking
B: 1 camping 2 hiking
3 cycling 4 explore 5 trips
6 guided

Exercise 2
A: 1 tired 2 cold 3 bored
4 lost
B: 1 dark 2 bored 3 lost
4 tired

Exercise 3
A: 1 left 2 met 3 was
4 stopped 5 bought
6 happened
B: 1 met 2 left 3 was
4 bought 5 read
6 happened

Exercise 4
A: 1 didn't eat 2 didn't swim
3 wasn't 4 didn't see
B: 1 weren't 2 didn't drink
3 didn't see 4 didn't swim

Exercise 5
A: 1 did 2 Did Anna go
3 didn't 4 were you 5 did
you arrive
B: 1 did 2 were you 3 Did Liz
take 4 didn't 5 did you
come

Exercise 6
A: 1 no problem 2 Can I
borrow 3 can't 4 Could I
5 Not now
B: 1 of course 2 Could I 3 no
4 Can I borrow 5 you can't

Language Test 4

Exercise 1
A: 1 blender 2 stick 3 remote
4 electric 5 console
6 toaster 7 microwave
B: 1 remote 2 console
3 microwave 4 blender
5 toaster 6 stick
7 toothbrush

Exercise 2
A: 1 off 2 battery 3 portable
4 touch screen 5 ringtone
B: 1 on 2 portable 3 battery
4 touch screen 5 ringtone

Exercise 3
A: 1 was reading 2 were
swimming 3 Were you and
Eva enjoying 4 weren't
having 5 were doing
B: 1 was playing 2 were
watching 3 Were you and
Brian relaxing 4 weren't
having 5 were studying

Exercise 4
A: 1 were sleeping 2 broke
3 started 4 was drying
B: 1 was running 2 heard
3 was having 4 broke

Exercise 5
A: 1 badly 2 carefully 3 fast
4 angrily
B: 1 fast 2 carefully 3 badly
4 happily

Exercise 6
A: 1 happened 2 hear
3 worried 4 What's
5 shame
B: 1 wrong 2 terrible 3 upset
4 shame 5 What

Language Test 5

Exercise 1
A: 1 headache 2 sore
3 runny 4 blocked
5 sneeze 6 cough
B: 1 headache 2 cough
3 sneeze 4 sore 5 runny
6 blocked

Exercise 2
A: 1 cut 2 bites 3 burn
4 bruise
B: 1 burn 2 bruise 3 cut
4 bites

Exercise 3
A: 1 heart 2 Blood 3 bones
4 brain
B: 1 bones 2 heart 3 brain
4 Blood

Exercise 4
A: 1 We don't have to water
2 Does Dora have to do
3 Mum has to work 4 Do
they have to study 5 John
doesn't have to walk
6 Where do you have to go
B: 1 You don't have to water
2 Does Phil have to help
3 Dad has to make 4 Do
we have to study 5 Celia
doesn't have to take
6 What do you have to do

Exercise 5
A: 1 should drink 2 shouldn't
go 3 Should I leave,
shouldn't 4 should put
B: 1 Should we put, should
2 shouldn't swim 3 should
drink, shouldn't sit

Exercise 6
A: 1 c 2 d 3 a 4 b 5 e
B: 1 a 2 e 3 d 4 b 5 c

Language Test 6

Exercise 1
A: 1 bowl 2 Add 3 mix
4 Bake 5 oven
B: 1 bowl 2 Add 3 mix
4 Bake 5 oven

Exercise 2
A: 1 tin 2 pan 3 mug
4 spoon, fork
B: 1 pot 2 knife 3 spoon
4 tin 5 glass

Exercise 3
A: 1 sour 2 sweet
3 disgusting 4 spicy
B: 1 salty 2 spicy 3 disgusting
4 sour

Exercise 4
A: 1 haven't cleaned 2 have
put 3 hasn't loaded 4 has
made 5 has left
B: 1 has made 2 hasn't put
3 has left 4 haven't cleaned
5 have loaded

Exercise 5
A: 1 A: Have they ever been
on TV? B: Yes, they have.
2 A: Has she bought the
vegetables? B: Yes, she has.
3 A: Have you ever eaten
Mexican food? B: No, I/we
haven't.
B: 1 A: Have you ever been
on TV? B: No, I/we haven't.
2 A: Have they ever eaten
pasta with pesto? B: No,
they haven't. 3 A: Has she
bought the fruit? B: Yes, she
has.

Exercise 6
A: 1 choose 2 don't mind
3 I'd like to 4 like 5 I'd
B: 1 don't mind 2 like 3 I'd
4 choose 5 I'd like to

Language Test 7

Exercise 1
A: 1 cottage 2 attic 3 village
4 block 5 floor 6 stairs
7 balcony
B: 1 cottage 2 village
3 attic 4 detached 5 city
6 ground 7 basement

Exercise 2
A: 1 sink 2 mirror 3 tap
4 cupboard
B: 1 cupboard 2 sink
3 drawer 4 mirror

Exercise 3
A: 1 out 2 up 3 for 4 out
B: 1 out 2 up 3 up 4 for

Exercise 4
A: 1 'm going 2 is Joe studying
4 's playing 4 Are Amy and
Fred coming 5 're moving
B: 1 'm taking 2 Is Tony doing
3 's meeting 4 Are Ben and
Sally study 5 're visiting

Exercise 5
A: 1 mustn't 2 must 3 must
4 mustn't 5 Can
B: 1 mustn't 2 Can 3 mustn't
4 must 5 can

Exercise 6
A: 1 That sounds 2 Are you
free 3 I'd love to 4 Can
you come 5 I can't
B: 1 That sounds 2 Would
you like 3 maybe next time
4 Are you free 5 I'd love to

Language Test 8

Exercise 1
A: 1 have 2 foreign 3 abroad
4 own 5 have
B: 1 be 2 foreign 3 abroad
4 own 5 have

Exercise 2
A: 1 hands 2 kissed 3 hug
4 visiting
B: 1 kissed 2 hug 3 hands
4 visiting

Exercise 3
A: 1 late 2 asks 3 interrupts
4 waits 5 polite
B: 1 late 2 interrupts 3 asks
4 turn 5 polite

Exercise 4
A: 1 won't get 2 Will you go
3 won't be 4 Will they win
5 will be 6 will you live
B: 1 won't be 2 will you live
3 Will you buy 4 won't arrive
5 Will they pass 6 will be

Exercise 5
A: 1 Why are 2 How often do
3 What were 4 Where did
5 When are 6 Who is
B: 1 What were 2 Where did
3 Why are 4 How often
does 5 When are 6 Who
did

Exercise 6
A: 1 That isn't 2 That's true
3 I don't think 4 That's what
5 I disagree
B: 1 I disagree 2 I don't think
3 That isn't 4 That's true
5 That's what

Skills Test 1&2

Exercise 1
A: 1 150 2 blue 3 medium
4 card 5 bookshop
B: 1 expensive 2 chemist's
3 19 4 cash 5 café

Exercise 2
A: 1 b 2 a 3 a 4 a 5 b
B: 1 b 2 b 3 b 4 a 5 a

Exercise 3
A: 1 c 2 f 3 d 4 e 5 a
B: 1 f 2 g 3 a 4 b 5 d

Exercise 4
A: 1 F 2 F 3 T 4 T 5 F
B: 1 T 2 F 3 F 4 F 5 T

Exercise 5
A: 1 At 2 enough 3 baker's
4 is 5 than
B: 1 Right 2 too 3 don't
4 greengrocer's 5 as

Exercise 6

Model text

On Saturdays I usually
get up at ten. I make my
bed and tidy my room.
After breakfast, I clear
the table and load the
dishwasher. Dad vacuums
the rooms and Mum
waters the plants. Then my
parents go shopping at
the supermarket. I usually
go with them and carry the
shopping bags to the car.
In the afternoon,
I hang out with my friends.
We sometimes go to the
cinema in the evening.

Answer key

Skills Test 3&4

Exercise 1
A: 1 Cathy's grandma 2 Yes, they did. 3 They explored the city. 4 In a café 5 He was on a boat trip.

B: 1 Yes, they did. 2 In a hotel (in the centre of the city) 3 They visited Grandma. 4 In a café 5 He was with his dad.

Exercise 2
A: 1 c 2 a 3 d 4 b 5 e
B: 1 e 2 d 3 a 4 c 5 b

Exercise 3
A: 1 h 2 f 3 e 4 a 5 d
B: 1 b 2 c 3 g 4 a 5 h

Exercise 4
A: 1 very hot 2 she was tired 3 fish 4 explored the city 5 walk

B: 1 very hot 2 they were hungry 3 salad 4 guided tour 4 any cars

Exercise 5
A: 1 was 2 oven 3 battery 4 portable 5 broke

B: 1 go 2 microwave 3 broke 4 battery 5 charger

Exercise 6
Model text

Last month, we visited my aunt and uncle in the country. It was a sunny day. Mum and Dad were sitting in the garden and talking to my aunt and uncle. My cousin and I were taking photos on my new smartphone. We were having fun. Suddenly, it started to rain. I was running into the house when I dropped my smartphone. The screen broke and the smartphone stopped working. I felt terrible.

Skills Test 5&6

Exercise 1
A: 1 c 2 a 3 c 4 c 5 b
B: 1 b 2 c 3 b 4 a 5 c

Exercise 2
A: 1 milk 2 Add 3 8 / eight 4 2 / two 5 sugar

B: 1 milk 2 bread 3 slice 4 2 / two 5 15 / fifteen

Exercise 3
A: 1 Why don't you lie down? / I think you should lie down. 2 Have you seen the doctor? 3 Would you like some tea? 4 Why don't you take a painkiller? 5 Do you have to do any homework tonight?

B: 1 Why don't you take a painkiller? 2 Have you seen the doctor? 3 Would you like some tea? / Why don't you drink some tea? 4 Would you like to lie down? 5 Do you have to get up early tomorrow?

Exercise 4
A: 1 She coughs. 2 He ate too much. 3 He has broken his arm. 4 She's in bed. 5 She's made some mint tea.

B: 1 She drinks tea and orange juice. 2 He ate too much yesterday. 3 He was skateboarding. 4 He's on the sofa. 5 They're having spaghetti and tomato sauce.

Exercise 5
A: 1 have 2 should 3 tin 4 mix 5 oven
B: 1 have 2 tin 3 should 4 oven 5 Bake

Exercise 6
Model text

When you have the flu, you feel terrible. You usually have a temperature and a headache. Sometimes you have a sore throat and a cough. You should see the doctor. You shouldn't go to school or do any sports. You should stay in bed and rest. Hot soup is good for you. You should also drink lots of water or warm tea.

Skills Test 7&8

Exercise 1
A: 1 In a drawer 2 Dad's 3 Last night 4 No, he didn't. 5 For a glass of water / Because he wanted a glass of water.

B: 1 On the bookcase 2 Mum's 3 Last night 4 A few minutes 5 No, he didn't.

Exercise 2
A: 1 F 2 F 3 T 4 F 5 T
B: 1 F 2 F 3 T 4 T 5 F

Exercise 3
A: 2 e 3 g 4 b 5 c 6 f
B: 2 d 3 f 4 c 5 a 6 g

Exercise 4
A: 1 from home 2 next to 3 cottage 4 the ground floor 5 are driving

B: 1 his computer 2 semi-detached 3 packing their things 4 the ground floor 5 school

Exercise 5
A: 1 Shake 2 late 3 turn 4 foreign 5 Call

B: 1 shake 2 Visit 3 late 4 interrupt 5 foreign

Exercise 6
Model text

When I finish school, I'll be a vet. I love animals and I think I'll be good at my job. I'll live in the country and work with farm animals. I'll also work with people's pets. My best friend will be an English teacher. He's very good at foreign languages. I love visiting other countries, so I'm sure I'll go abroad. I'd love to see Africa and South America. I hope I'll be more patient in the future.

Mid-Year Test

Exercise 1
A: 1 Hang 2 list 3 Check 4 baker's 5 greengrocer's

B: 1 Put 2 bag 3 receipt 4 greengrocer's 5 baker's

Exercise 2
A: 1 hiking 2 get 3 bored 4 boat 5 messy

B: 1 bored 2 trips 3 explore 4 get 5 guided

Exercise 3
A: 1 apps 2 ringtone 3 charger 4 remote 5 console

B: 1 charger 2 ringtone 3 apps 4 console 5 remote

Exercise 4
A: 1 'm looking 2 need 3 doesn't like 4 's waiting 5 Do you spend

B: 1 want 2 'm trying 3 doesn't need 4 's waiting 5 Do you spend

Exercise 5
A: 1 the funniest 2 organised 3 better 4 big 5 the most stylish

B: 1 worse 2 the happiest 3 the most stylish 4 big 5 patient

Exercise 6
A: 1 came 2 Did 3 doing 4 was looking 5 have

B: 1 got 3 doing 3 Did 4 play 5 was buying

Exercise 7
A: 1 bossy 2 her bed 3 electric toothbrush 4 4.99 5 in cash 6 sports shop

B: 1 messy 2 to Italy 3 electric toothbrush 4 6.99 5 by card 6 Mum

Exercise 8
A: 1 that's fine 2 Can I 3 What size 4 Here you are 5 Could you, busy 6 upset, a shame

B: 1 What size 2 Could you, busy 3 Do you need 4 look, to hear that 5 Can I 6 Here you are

Exercise 9
A: 1 F 2 T 3 F 4 T 5 T 6 F
B: 1 T 2 F 3 F 4 T 5 F 6 T

End-of-Year Test

Exercise 1
A: 1 village 2 business 3 shake 4 water 5 out

B: 1 village 2 own 3 hang 4 rubbish 5 shake

Exercise 2
A: 1 queue 2 try 3 oven 4 peel 5 up

B: 1 oven 2 peel 3 up 4 queue 5 try

Exercise 3
A: 1 blender 2 forks 3 sink 4 ringtone 5 drawer

B: 1 mirror 2 drawer 3 spoons 4 blender 5 battery

Exercise 4
A: 1 left 2 I'm trying 3 I'm playing 4 didn't water 5 were exploring

B: 1 We're meeting 2 was waiting 3 went 4 didn't tidy 5 They're trying

Exercise 5
A: 1 Have you ever stayed 2 will be 3 have broken 4 has made 5 will you do

B: 1 Have you ever visited 2 have broken 3 will be 4 will you live 5 has baked

Exercise 6
A: 1 tall enough 2 carefully 3 have to 4 mustn't 5 worst

B: 1 have to 2 funniest 3 strong enough 4 well 5 can

Exercise 7
A: 1 T 2 T 3 T 4 F 5 F 6 T
B: 1 F 2 T 3 F 4 T 5 T 6 T

Exercise 8
A: 1 b 2 g 3 f 4 h 5 a 6 e 7 d 8 c
B: 1 g 2 a 3 d 4 h 5 f 6 e 7 c 8 b

Exercise 9
A: 1 chores 2 hug 3 invite 4 money 5 neighbourhood 6 park

B: 1 happy 2 hug 3 neighbours 4 food 5 streets 6 trees